47999

DATE DUE			

D1551137

POWER ALONG THE HUDSON

ALSO BY ALLAN R. TALBOT

The Mayor's Game

E. P. Dutton & Co., Inc.   *New York*   1972

POWER ALONG

The Storm King Case and

ALLAN R. TALBOT

THE HUDSON

the Birth of Environmentalism

HD
9685
U7
C168

Published simultaneously in Canada by Clarke, Irwin & Company
Limited, Toronto and Vancouver
SBN: 0-525-18250-0
Library of Congress Catalog Card Number: 71-158609
Designed by The Etheredges

47999

For Kate

CONTENTS

POWER ALONG THE HUDSON

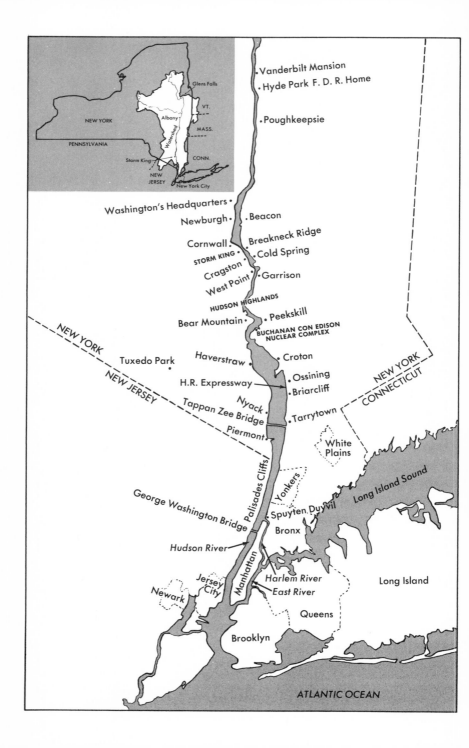

INTRODUCTION

In 1963 a simple question came up that seemed to warrant a quick answer: Should Consolidated Edison, the private utility serving New York City and adjacent Westchester County, receive a Federal Power Commission license to construct a hydroelectric plant at the base of Storm King Mountain, forty miles north of New York City in the Hudson Highlands?

Given the shabby appearance of some of the Hudson River shoreline from Glens Falls in upstate New York down to the abandoned piers of Manhattan's West Side, the question might easily have been answered with another: Why not?

1

Con Edison proposed to remove a portion of Storm King Mountain to provide a site for a pumping station and power-house. A tunnel forty feet wide and two miles long would be bored through the mountain up to a reservoir with a capacity of 8 billion gallons. River water would be pumped into the reservoir at night or on weekends, when Con Edison's New York City base generators operate below capacity. When other utilities wished to purchase electricity from the company, or when Con Edison required auxiliary power during the peak demand periods, water in the reservoir would be released through the tunnel, its flow activating the blades of the riverside power-house. The project, termed a pumped-storage hydroelectric plant, was to be the largest of its kind in the world.

The anticipated tax revenues of the Con Edison project encouraged the support of the majority of people living in Cornwall, a town of about 10,000 people located on the northern slope of Storm King. Cornwall, like many river towns, has seen better days, and its officials seemed prepared to deal with anyone who might help their tax base. The plant project was opposed by a minority of people living in and around Cornwall, including weekenders who have second homes in the highlands and who place a premium on the natural beauty and quiet of the area. More numerous were the opponents across the river in Cold Spring, Garrison, and Philipstown. They did not like the idea of looking at the plant and its transmission lines and would not, of course, benefit from its tax contribution.

Discussions over the project departed from the normal script of land-use conflicts in 1964, when people beyond the vicinity of Storm King heard of Con Edison's plans. Joining with local opponents, an emergency coalition of individuals and various hiking, garden, conservation, and sporting clubs closed ranks to fight the plant. They called themselves the Scenic Hudson Preservation Conference and dispatched representatives to Washington, D.C., to oppose the Federal Power Commission license. Lawyers for Con Edison, as well as the FPC staff, were surprised to see these outsiders enter the commission's hearing room, which seldom draws a crowd. The puzzlement turned to chagrin as a routine license application gradually attracted regional and then national opposition.

The Scenic Hudson coalition raised every conceivable objection: the plant would leak and might cause an earthquake; fish would be sucked into the pumping station and destroyed. Scenic Hudson suggested that there were better methods and other sites Con Edison could use to supplement its energy production. But the central argument was that the plant would destroy the scenic beauty of the mountain and might well introduce other industrial development to the highlands.

Although these arguments failed to impress the FPC, which granted Con Edison a construction license in the spring of 1965, they did arouse the interest of diverse groups. In the fall of 1964 a flotilla of small boats surrounded the river side of Storm King in symbolic defense of its integrity. Sports fishermen along the river protested against Con Edison by periodically turning off the electric lights and appliances in their homes. Folk singer Pete Seeger composed ballads about the mountain and for the first time in his career received the applause of conservative Republicans.

Defending Storm King became a national cause. Celebrities were drawn to it, like touring statesmen visiting the Berlin Wall. Robert Kennedy, Aaron Copland, James Cagney, and

Brooks Atkinson had very little in common except for their announced opposition to Con Edison's project. Among the celebrities who publicly supported it were Edward Teller, Robert Moses, and Laurance Rockefeller.

A federal appeals court boosted Scenic Hudson's cause in December 1965 by remanding the FPC license and instructing the agency to give scenic factors equal weight with power requirements in its license reviews. The court also ruled that conservation groups have the legal standing to protect the public's interest in natural beauty under the Federal Power Act. Related court opinions quickly followed, culminating in a 1970 decision on the Hudson River Expressway—a subsequent controversy related to that of Storm King—which sustained the right of any "responsible representative" to sue in the federal courts to protect the public interest in the environment. These were landmark decisions.

The Sierra Club, the Audubon Society, and the Izaak Walton League are among the national conservation organizations that support Scenic Hudson. They quite naturally regard the 1965 court decision as a milestone and often characterize the Storm King struggle as the conservation fight of the century. The utility industry, on the other hand, sees the case as the beginning of the nation's power crisis. The utilities feel that the court's decision on Storm King has encouraged groups, some acting only on narrow interests, to block the construction of badly needed power plants. As for Con Edison, its executives claim that during the summer crises of 1969 and 1970 their power problems were directly attributable to the legal delays of the Storm King project.

Aside from dramatizing the conflicts between urban power

INTRODUCTION

needs and natural beauty, the battle over Storm King Mountain created new interest in and appreciation of the Hudson River, which like most American rivers has been badly treated. Before Con Edison's Storm King proposal, there had never been any widespread interest in the river's ecology or its future as a wild-life resource. The suggestion that fish would be sucked into the plant was doubly startling since few people were aware that fish still swam in the Hudson.

The debate over Storm King revealed that very little was known about how the river worked and survived. It also demonstrated that there was considerable official confusion over jurisdictions, and that there were no satisfactory arrangements for planning and regulating river uses and resolving conflicts such as the one caused by the proposed power plant. Beginning in 1966 the institutional and political giants of the Hudson tried to sort out their responsibilities while Congress passed numerous laws to protect the natural, historical, and scenic resources of the Hudson. In 1967 the Department of the Interior, with the backing of New Jersey, which borders on a portion of the river, began advocating a federal-state compact agency. New York's Governor Nelson Rockefeller resisted, saying that the Hudson was basically New York property. Meanwhile the mayors of river towns in both states said that control over riverside land should remain with them. In the midst of this tug of war Con Edison and some other major industrial users of the Hudson pledged to improve the river and to curb their abuses. The river disputes that contributed so significantly to environmental law now became enmeshed in the politics of the environment.

In the fall of 1971 the cause of all this activity, the debate over the proposed power plant on Storm King Mountain, finally headed toward a resolution. Following the 1965 instructions of the appeals court, the FPC reopened its hearings in 1966, recording 19,000 pages of new testimony, and then, in 1970, reissued the construction license to Con Edison. Scenic Hudson again appealed, only this time its lawyers asked the federal court to set the license aside rather than remand it for further hearings, as the court had done in 1965. The court refused. Two of the three judges concluded that the FPC had followed the 1965 instructions. Con Edison was authorized to proceed with construction. In 1972 the U.S. Supreme Court refused to hear Scenic Hudson's appeal of this decision.

Although the simple question of 1963 had to wait until 1972 to get the predictable answer, the intervening years saw the birth of broader questions about American values and priorities, expressed in large part by the environmental movement born on Storm King Mountain. To examine those questions, one must start with the oldest and leading figure in the story: the billion-year-old mountain itself.

THE MOUNTAIN

Storm King Mountain and the Hudson Valley represent a deep slice of the American past. The history of the region is more than just interesting background; it offers some explanations for the conflict and confusion that have arisen along the river since the power plant was first proposed. Though the battle over Storm King broke out in 1963, it had been building for three centuries.

The Hudson has played a key role in many periods of American history. The valley was one of the first sections of North America to be explored by Europeans. In the seventeenth century the Dutch seized it from the Indians and began to colonize it. The British then took the valley from the Dutch and hastened its development.

The colonists severed their European ties during the Revolutionary War, which many historians feel was decided when the revolutionaries succeeded in beating off British attempts to control the Hudson Highlands. The fiercest fighting in that campaign took place in the immediate vicinity of Storm King Mountain.

Following the war, the Hudson Valley area gave rise to distinctive American inventions, architecture, arts, and personalities. The nation's first major public works project, the Erie Canal, linked the Hudson to the Great Lakes. The Hudson inspired the nation's first writers and landscape artists. The locomotive and the steamship were invented along the river, and out of these inventions soon came the national industries that produced the robber barons, many of whom got their start and flaunted their wealth along the Hudson. Many of the nation's foremost public leaders also left their mark on the river, including DeWitt Clinton, Martin Van Buren, Franklin D. Roosevelt, Alfred E. Smith, and Robert Moses, to name only a few.

The topography of Storm King suggests that there is much more involved in the recent argument than whether a power company should reshape a mountain. The predominate granite of Storm King gives it a light gray cast tinged occasionally with the faint pink and green of quartz, feldspar, and mica. The surface is coarse and rocky, with far fewer trees than other formations in the Hudson Highlands, such as Bear Mountain or Dundenberg, and at 1,300 feet it is the tallest of the highlands mountains bordering directly on the river.

THE MOUNTAIN

The numerous scars on Storm King create a scenic detraction, but they reveal the mountain's history. The most visible cut is a two-lane highway about one-third of the way up from the river. The Storm King Highway was built in 1876 from Cornwall, on the northern slope, to the West Point Military Academy, five miles south. Before the highway was built, the main entrance to Cornwall was the town dock. During the nineteenth century the Hudson was the major resort area for the northeastern United States, and the principal visitors to the area were vacationers and travelers.

Between the construction of the highway in 1876 and the advent of more daring mountain sculptures such as the Stony Gorge Dam, built in California in 1926, American guidebook writers often referred to the Storm King road as an engineering wonder of the world. By 1930 the highway had been demoted to an engineering wonder of the northeast. Today the few travelers who still use the highway seem interested less in how men managed to cut a road out of Storm King granite than in painting their initials on it.

The mountain overwhelms the river, making it impossible for an observer at ground level to see its full size. From a boat or the east bank of the river Storm King seems like a small, impressive dome rising directly from the Hudson. But from an airplane it is clear that the mountain actually has a mile-long back and resembles an immense beached whale, with the highway forming its mouth.

In the early nineteenth century Americans called this impressive formation Butter Hill. A Con Edison attorney once remarked that if the old name had remained, his client would have had far less trouble claiming it for a power plant. His legal adversaries agree that it would have been difficult to raise money or excitement over a place called Butter Hill.

Nathaniel Parker Willis, who lived in Cornwall toward the end of a migratory literary career, suggested the name Storm King in 1850. Willis came upon this choice while observing, as one still may, that on cloudy days the top of the mountain often disappears in mist. "When the white cloud beard descends upon his breast (as if with a nod forward of his majestic head)," Willis wrote, "there is sure to be a rainstorm before night."

The name Butter Hill seems to have been a corruption of the early German name, Buttel Hill. Buttel means guard or bailiff, and by mispronouncing the end of the word Americans also destroyed the early settlers' idea that the mountain was the northern guard to the Hudson Highlands. Eighteenth-century navigators were both impressed by and afraid of Buttel Hill. According to legend it was inhabited by little men who blew on trumpets in order to topple the masts of ships sailing through the gorge between Storm King and Breakneck Ridge on the east bank. The basis of such a story can still be appreciated by sailors, for the winds are erratic in the gorge and often howl in mysterious ways.

Later Americans showed little awe of the mountain. In the nineteenth century the West Point Foundry, located across the river and to the south in Cold Spring, routinely tested cannon balls by firing them into the southern side of the mountain. No one was greatly upset by the creases, nor was there much stir in 1880 over a proposal by some Poughkeepsie businessmen to construct a suspension bridge across the Storm King gorge. By land standards of the nineteenth century, Storm King was worthless property: too steep for development, too rugged for farming, too thin in forest growth, and as it turned out inappropriate for a bridge. The project died when no one could figure out what a traveler might do upon reaching the other side.

The recorded history of the mountain goes back to the 1609 voyage of Henry Hudson. One of the most perilous moments in that unhappy trip occurred when Hudson's ship, the *Half Moon,* passed through the gorge. A severe windstorm battered the boat, adding greatly to the insecurities of Hudson's already touchy crew.

Hudson was an Englishman employed by the Dutch East India Company to determine whether the river might lead to India. That idea is not as ridiculous as one might now suppose. The waters of the Hudson are tidal to Troy and are brackish through the highlands up to a point just south of Poughkeepsie, about eighty miles north of Manhattan. It was not unreasonable to assume that the waterway might join with another ocean.

On Sunday morning, September 6, 1609, Hudson anchored his ship in the lower bay of New York Harbor, dispatching an advance party of five to take soundings at the mouth of the river. According to the logbook of Robert Juet, a mate on Hudson's expedition, the day was clear and warm as the men rowed off. By noon, when they were expected to return, it had clouded over, and by evening it was raining steadily. At dawn the following day the rain stopped and the sky cleared, but there was still no sign of the missing men. At noon their small boat finally appeared and pulled alongside the *Half Moon.* Two of the men were badly wounded. A third had an arrow lodged in his throat. He was dead.

Nonetheless, Hudson ordered his crew to sail into the harbor for the trip up river. The Indians of the valley were both frightened and intrigued by the huge ship. The more memorable encounters between the two cultures occurred in the Storm King vicinity. At the southern entrance to the highlands, for instance, one Indian climbed aboard secretly, investigated the stern section of the ship, and decided to make off with some trifles including Juet's pillow and two of his shirts. He was detected as he jumped overboard. Some of the crew rowed after him, cut off his hand, retrieved the stolen goods, and let the Indian drown. North of Storm King the expedition came across "loving people," as Juet described them, including an old man who visited the *Half Moon* on several occasions bringing with him food, his wife, and then some young girls. By the time the ship reached what is now the town of Hudson, about fifty miles north of Storm King, the Europeans had introduced the local Indians to wine during an all-night party which, Juet stressed, was mainly a test of the local populace to determine "whether there was any treachery in them."

For Hudson the twenty-seven-day trip was a disappointment. The river was navigable for only about 125 miles, ending at what is now Albany. The river turned out to be merely an estuary of the Atlantic Ocean and led nowhere. In his report to the directors of the Dutch East India Company, Hudson stressed the positive. The river, he said, had beautiful scenery, pleasant trees, and sweet smells, although its native population was unpredictable. But company directors were interested only in the river's terminus, and they dismissed the report. In 1610 Hudson embarked on another North American expedition from which he never returned. A mutinous crew set him adrift in a rowboat in the North Atlantic.

Another organization, the Dutch West India Company,

settled the Hudson Valley. In 1624 Peter Minuit purchased a large island at the mouth of the river from the Manhattan Indians under terms that later became national folklore. The Dutch West India Company also established the basic land policies under which the Hudson Valley was expropriated from the Indians and then divided among Europeans. The physical effects of these policies, particularly the fact that the Hudson Valley remains a largely unsettled region in the heart of the Boston-Washington megalopolis, may still be observed.

The legal basis for the Dutch West India Company's land program was the 1629 Charter of Freedoms and Exemptions, which offered valley land to buyers in sections as large as they could cultivate. At the urging of an Amsterdam merchant named Kiliaen Van Rensselaer, he and his fellow company directors were entitled to up to twenty-five miles of river bank if they set up their own colony of at least fifty settlers within four years. The owner of these tracts, called a patroon, had complete control over his land and settlers. Eventually five patroonships were established, the largest being Rensselaerswyck, located on both sides of the river in the Albany area.

The object of the patroonships was to overcome the marketing problems of selling wilderness to civilized customers by making it an attractive business proposition. There were not many buyers. When the British took over the valley in 1664 and replaced the patroonship system with their more generous manorial grants, only 8,000 Europeans had settled there.

By the middle of the eighteenth century the valley had been divided into enormous manorial tracts under the ownership of the more prominent families of the colony, including the Van Cortlands, Van Rensselaers, Livingstons, Philipses, and

Morrises. Storm King and the Hudson Highlands received little attention. Although the Philipse family staked a claim to the east bank of the highlands, they did little with it. Like other landlords, they were interested primarily in the level areas of the valley, where land could be rented for farming.

The Indians of the Hudson Valley were severely victimized by the European land programs and became the Hudson's first environmental casualties. Some Indians became domestic servants and slaves on the manors. Others huddled in the forests, sometimes striking back in revenge. Most Indian raids occurred on the Storm King side of the river, where the valley's few family-owned farms were located. The manors, on the better protected east bank, were less frequently attacked.

The Indians in the Hudson Highlands were members of the Leni-Lenape or Delaware branch of the Algonkian-speaking tribes. The Leni-Lenapes settled portions of the lower Hudson Valley in the year 1000 and were the most peaceful and least migratory of all the Indians of New York. The Indians became more bellicose up river, beginning first with the Wappinger Indians in the central Hudson area and then with the Mohawks, an Iroquois tribe, farther north. The Mohawks, the most durable and strongest of the Hudson Valley tribes, were raiding their downriver brothers well before the Europeans arrived. The present north-south highways along the river follow the Mohawks' warpaths.

The Europeans had better weapons, more fighters, and greater unity than the Indians. Seizure of the Hudson Valley was swift, as was the downfall of the Indians who inhabited it. Yet commercial development of the river valley was slow. Even as late as the American Revolution, most of the river was the same primitive wilderness that Henry Hudson explored. In the summer the valley was oppressively hot and humid compared with Europe. Insects and poisonous plants were numerous, and yellow fever was one of several mysterious and fatal ailments that rose from the wild to kill the settlers. Winter brought isolation and often starvation. From December to spring the river was usually frozen, stranding both squire and farmer. European settlers were often frightened by the Hudson River, and their fears gave rise to legends about mountaintop gremlins, headless horsemen, and of course the possibility that a man wandering in the wilder portions of the river might be put to sleep for twenty years.

While the Europeans were united in their fear of the Indian and the wilderness he represented, they were frequently at odds with one another. The Hudson River manor lords fared well, but their tenants were miserable. The farmers could not vote and could not own the homes they built or the fields they worked. The manor lords held durable leases and retained the value of the improvements made by the tenants.

The tenants' struggle to gain ownership of the land they worked began peacefully in the courts. Some tenants sought to purchase the land they leased from the manor lords by negotiating sales agreements with the Indians. The agreements recognized the Indians as rightful owners of manor lands and were therefore a profound legal challenge to the original Dutch and British land grants. The colonial courts were hardly the proper place to resolve such an issue. The deepest legal challenge concerning land policies had been a rash of suits among grantees over the alignment of their properties. It seems that the colonial governors were often imprecise about boundaries when they gave land away. Not surprisingly, the colonial judges declared the sales agreements between the tenants and the Indians invalid.

Failure of the legal strategy led to warfare. In the spring of 1766 a tenant revolt broke out on the Philipse manor. A brigade of farmers led by William Prendergast roamed the countryside, beating up rent collectors and judges who had arrested and imprisoned delinquent tenants. The high point of the insurgency was a raid on the jail at Poughkeepsie, where Prendergast released the prisoners and announced that the rebels would attack Manhattan. The band was surrounded and captured before it got to the Bronx.

After Prendergast's trial, in which he was sentenced to be tortured, hanged, and quartered, the colonial governor sensed that the rebel leader might become a martyr. When Prendergast's wife began making speeches pleading for her husband's life and outlining the evils of the manor system, he was released, and he and his family later left for Tennessee.

During the Revolutionary War the British tried unsuccessfully to use the Hudson to drive a north-south wedge between the colonies, and the highlands were the scene of fierce fighting, particularly in the West Point and Constitution Island areas. George Washington directed the campaigns from Newburgh, within sight of Storm King Mountain. On the east bank of the highlands the Philipse family remained loyal to the king. The Philipse tenants therefore helped Washington defend the highlands. If the Philipse family had supported the colonies, it is likely that their tenants would have helped the British side, and the war might have had a different outcome.

With the exception of the Philipse manor, which was broken up and distributed as bounty to returning officers, most of the manors survived the Revolution. During the first two decades of the nineteenth century the jails of the valley were filled with thousands of debtors. Suffrage was still restricted to men of property, and the tenant farmers resumed their guerrilla warfare. In New York City a radical intelligentsia composed of immigrant social idealists—including Francis Wright and Robert Evans from Scotland and George Evans from England —preached extensive land and labor reforms. Evans courted the tenant farmers, trying to weld their revolt into a national movement for land redistribution.

Yet by 1850 many of the sources of discontent were gone, and a second bloody revolution had not occurred. Business was booming, and a new, native-born middle class was being elected to public office by newly franchised voters. Alexis de Tocqueville was one of many European scholars and journalists who traveled to America to determine how this transformation had been achieved without the violence that occurred in other nations. One recurring theme in de Tocqueville's writing is the role of open land in the rise of American democracy. Later, American writers argued that the open frontier offered an escape valve for economic discontent and encouraged the rise of distinctively American styles and institutions.

But in the early nineteenth century, although the Hudson Valley retained some frontier characteristics, its architecture, customs, and social and economic institutions were basically conservative and European, as were its ruling patriarchs. The Americanization of the Hudson had to wait until 1825, when the Hudson's first major engineering project was completed. That project, far greater in scope and more daring than anything built or proposed since, including Con Edison's Storm King plant, can help us to understand America's infatuation with large-scale construction.

THE CANAL

The suggestion of an east-west canal running from the Hudson across the New York territory to Lake Erie was first made in 1724 by the surveyor general to the colonial governor. Thereafter a succession of governors considered the idea, for a navigable inland waterway would spur development in the Mohawk Valley, where many of the governors were handing out land grants. But the intrigues of the Iroquois in the area and Britain's continuing struggles with the French caused each of the governors to dismiss the project as unrealistic.

Interest in canal construction revived during the Revolutionary War. While many of the Founding Fathers were planning or fighting the war by day, they were discussing canals at night. George Washington found it an appealing subject and was especially fond of a plan to construct a canal between the Potomac and Ohio rivers after the war. In 1777, not the best year for the colonies, Benjamin Franklin was actually completing a report on European canals.

This optimistic and enthusiastic interest in canals was caused by the need to make the interior wilderness accessible, but Franklin's report listed other reasons, as well. "Rivers are ungovernable things," he wrote. "Canals are quiet and very manageable." For Franklin a canal was not only a form of transportation but an assertion of man's superiority over nature. He was impressed, for example, by the European practice of building canals alongside rivers, with "no other use being made of the rivers than to supply occasionally the waste of waters in the canal."

Of all the postwar projects, the Erie Canal promised to be the biggest battle between America and nature. Its proposed 350-mile alignment crossed granite mountains, swamps, and other rugged terrain. The Europeans, highly skilled in canal construction, had not built a longer or more difficult waterway.

The magnificent scale and challenge of the project were its principal attractions to the postwar leaders of New York State. Gouverneur Morris, a prominent canal advocate, conveyed their excitement.

Can you bring your imagination to realize this scene? . . .
Hundreds of large ships will in no distant period bound on
the billows of those inland seas. At this point commences a

*navigation of more than a thousand miles. Shall I lead
your astonishment to the verge of incredulity?*

Morris' prose suggests disregard for such details as how the
canal could be financed and built. By the opening of the nineteenth century the political obstacles seemed at least as great as
the engineering problems. European financiers, dismayed by the
lack of engineering expertise in America, refused to back the
project. Even President Thomas Jefferson, a dauntless builder-ar-
chitect, dismissed New York's request for federal aid. "It is
nothing short of madness to think of it," wrote Jefferson. It is
not clear, however, whether he was referring to the size of the
canal or to the ability of New York's federalists—such landed
aristocrats as Morris, Van Rensselaer, Livingston, and Jay—to
build it.

The skepticism of President Jefferson and the European
investors meant that New York would have to build the canal
with its own money. It was not enough for the patricians to be
infatuated by the canal; taxpaying farmers, businessmen, and
wage earners had to support it too. There had to be something
in it for them.

The canal was a major issue in the politics of postwar New
York State, which were at least as complex as they are today.
There were many divergent and competing groups. Control of a
new state government was the prize. The canal project floundered in the political confusion. Someone had yet to emerge
who would appreciate the canal's potential as "pork barrel," a
statewide project that offered something for everyone and that
could therefore unite the disparate electorate around a single
issue.

The political prince appeared in 1816. His name: DeWitt Clinton. Clinton had the necessary political equipment for his day. He was energetic and big enough to be seen in a crowd, and he had a booming voice that could be heard from a distance. Within a span of fourteen years he had served as a state Senator, U.S. Senator, Lieutenant Governor of New York, and mayor of New York City. In 1812 he was the Republican nominee for President.

His skill as an infighter made him one of the few New Yorkers who could take on Aaron Burr, the Mephistopheles of early American politics. Clinton fought and defeated Burr for control of the Tammany Society, a New York political organization. The two men also battled over the Council of Appointments, which dispensed job patronage in the state. The council conflict was settled in a duel between Clinton and one of Burr's aides. Clinton took over the council by shooting the aide in the leg.

Clinton's loss to James Madison in the 1812 presidential election was a major political setback. When he returned to resume his job as mayor of New York City, then an appointive post, he was regarded as a has-been and a rather dangerous one at that. In 1815 his fellow Republican, Governor Daniel Thompkins, refused to reappoint him, apparently sensing that Clinton now had his sights set on the Governor's job.

At this low point in his career—without a job, a power base, or even an issue from which he could make a comeback —Clinton discovered the Erie Canal project. In 1811 he had served on a canal study committee, but his participation had been neither distinguished nor significant. Virtually every public figure in New York had served on some canal committee, for the project stands as one of the most thoroughly studied in the history of public works.

Governor Thompkins' agreement in 1816 to make Clinton the chairman of yet another canal committee suggests that Thompkins may have felt that the project was virtually a dead issue and that the man whom he had just removed as mayor would have little chance to revive it or himself politically.

Clinton stomped the Hudson and Mohawk valleys, speaking in towns and hamlets that no other canal advocate had visited previously. He directed his talks to the specific interests of his audience. For farmers, he claimed, the canal would mean quicker shipments. For carpenters it promised barge construction, for businessmen new markets, for laborers more work. In the northeastern corner of the state, which would be unaffected by the Erie, Clinton proposed a canal joining the Hudson with Lake Champlain.

In New York City he reassured merchants who expressed fear that their taxes would pay for most of the canal. No, said Clinton, he would see to it that special assessments were levied on upstate towns along the route of the canal. He dealt with financing questions in a brochure that he distributed around the state. He budgeted $7 million for the canal, a monumental public outlay in those days. But Clinton promised that the cost, when compared to the return, would appear modest. The Hudson would become a national river. New towns would rise inland, the project would pay for itself in user fees and assessments, and everyone would make money.

These persuasive arguments, delivered with sales techniques that suggest contemporary political campaigns, united enough people behind the project for the Erie to become the central issue in New York by 1817. The legislature backed it, and Clinton secured the Republican nomination for Governor and went on to win. Work on the canal began on July 5, 1817.

The Erie was built the way World War II was won, with very little finesse. Explosives and hand shovels were the basic tools by which mountains, forests, swamps, and streams were blasted, leveled, cut, and drained. Thousands of laborers worked on it, many of them imported from Ireland. There were mistakes, delays, and numerous accidents. Engineering skills were for the most part derived from rather than invested in the project, which now appears to have been an immense job-training program. Some laborers, such as John Jervis, later became America's first civil engineers. Despite the obstacles and against the odds, in October 1825 the new nation completed digging its great 350-mile ditch from Troy on the Hudson River to Lake Erie.

Governor Clinton's political fortunes fluctuated with those of the canal. When, in 1822, the canal was beset with delays and public apathy, Clinton was dumped by the Republicans. He formed a new organization—the People's party—and resumed his canal campaign of 1816. In 1823 he was reelected.

Cannon exploded and thousands cheered as the resilient Clinton waved from the first boat to appear in Manhattan after a trip through central New York. The celebration was a national event and a personal triumph. When the boat reached the harbor Clinton picked up a barrel of water from Lake Erie and poured it majestically into the Atlantic, not far from the point where Hudson's *Half Moon* had first anchored more than 200 years earlier.

Gouverneur Morris was no politician, but he proved to be a prophet—the effect of the canal was "astonishing to the point of incredulity." Smallmouth bass from Lake Erie were swimming in the Hudson and the waters of the Atlantic now connected to Rome, New York. No future emerging nation would ever match the drama, audacity, and scale of this canal. The pride of accomplishment fostered America's growing love affair with vast engineering projects; the practical benefits gave it permanence.

If, as de Tocqueville observed, God gave Americans an abundance of frontier land where new institutions could grow, the Erie gave them the means to get there. That effect was quickly seen in the disintegration of the manors, where both lord and radical lost a captive audience. The tenants embarked on the canal, stopping with other settlers to begin new lives in hamlets that eventually became cities: Utica, Rochester, Buffalo, Cleveland, and Chicago. The Hudson, no longer a wild river, was a national highway.

The dramatic changes are portrayed in the travelers' journals of the early nineteenth century. The observations before and after 1825 differ so much that it is hard to believe the writers are describing the same river. Isaac Weld, traveling in the summer of 1796, was appalled by the primitive conditions of the Hudson. With the exception of his first sight of Manhattan, "beautifully wooded, the trees almost dipping in the water," Weld's journal is filled with unpleasant comments about such annoying conditions as mosquitoes, windstorms, the lack of civilization along the shore, and the ugliness of Albany. "I shall leave it without a sigh, and without entertaining the slightest wish to revisit it," Weld concluded.

THE CANAL

John Lambert, another British visitor, was not as harsh, but the impressions he recorded in his journal in the fall of 1807 reflect shock and disappointment, particularly over the frozen condition of the river by early November. The ice deprived Lambert of a long-awaited trip from Troy to New York City on Robert Fulton's steamship, which was iced in at the dock. Lambert carriaged south to Hudson, where he boarded a sloop for his journey. Lambert found the river to be quaint. "In several places along the shore," he wrote, "are elegant mansions and country seats belonging to the principal persons of New York." But with the exception of "several little towns and villages along the waterside," Lambert reported, there was nothing much to see except wilderness and an occasional Indian.

Ten years after the opening of the canal the journal of Freeman Hunt describes a bustling valley. Newburgh had three new brick plants and its first brewery, under the ownership of J. Beveridge. Poughkeepsie had a new silk plant employing "one thousand young ladies ready to enter the blissful state of matrimony." Albany was a boom town, as was Troy, which had doubled its population since the opening of the canal and now boasted, in addition to many new mills and factories, four banks and two insurance companies.

In 1837 Captain Frederick Marryat, an English novelist, concluded his observations of the Hudson by wondering: "Where is the race of red men who hunted on its banks or fished and paddled in its streams?" Marryat explained the disappearance with some fundamental Christian philosophy:

No portion of this world was ever intended to remain for ages untenanted. Beasts of prey and noxious reptiles are permitted to exist in the wild and uninhabited regions until they are swept away by the broad streams of Civilization, which, as it pours along, drives them from hold to hold. So it is with more savage nations.

Free enterprise flourished in the valley between 1825 and the Civil War. One year before the opening of the canal Governor Clinton broke up the Livingston-Fulton steamboat monopoly with new laws making it possible for anyone to enter the business. A new breed of captain entrepreneurs came along and the graceful sloops of the Hudson bounced about in the wake of fast-moving steamers.

Major landing points were soon marked by a scarcity of timber in the surrounding hillsides, for wood was the fuel of the early steamers. About twenty-five cords were burned in a fifteen-hour trip between Albany and New York. The landings were lively spots, known for their boozing and wenching. "The landing is a nest of bad company," wrote Willis of the Cornwall waterfront beneath Storm King Mountain, ". . . and the farmers are moving away from it for a higher moral atmosphere."

An added attraction was impromptu steamboat races. The owner captains felt compelled to demonstrate their superiority over the competition, even if it meant passing a scheduled stop or scaring the wits out of passengers. To increase speed, a captain would jam the safety valve on his boiler and, if necessary, stuff deck chairs and other loose furnishings into the furnace. When a racing steamer crashed into the rocks off the Riverdale section of the Bronx in 1858, resulting in seventy deaths, federal and state laws were enacted to curb the races.

The fishing industry of the Hudson also expanded after the

opening of the canal. Bass, shad, and shellfish from the river were transported east and west. Caviar from the sturgeon of the Hudson became America's leading export to Russia by the middle of the nineteenth century.

The rapid growth of shipping briefly retarded railroad development in the Hudson Valley, despite the fact that the nation's first locomotive had been assembled by John Stevens on the New Jersey bank of the Hudson in 1823. Both steamboat and canal interests in New York fought the public subsidies for railroads that were commonplace in other states. But the new competition would not be denied. Numerous river towns and cities began building their own railroads with local backers.

The first line, the Mohawk and Hudson, appeared in 1831. Like all the early railroads it was built simply to connect adjacent cities with some speed and reliability. The Mohawk and Hudson connected Albany to Schenectady. The train consisted of three carriages adjusted to run on wooden track and was pulled by a tiny locomotive called the DeWitt Clinton. A second line was built in 1833 joining Albany to Saratoga, which was becoming a major resort area.

The trains for the Saratoga run looked more like the passenger cars of today. Designed by the Gilbert, Veazie, and Eaton Company of Troy, they were twenty-four feet long and eight feet wide, and were divided into three compartments. The cars were made of wood and were painted yellow. The sides were embellished with paintings of famous war heroes framed in a border of rose, pink, and gold.

Small lines promoted and run by local businessmen proliferated. By 1845 there were ten intercity lines between Albany and Buffalo, and passengers traveling through central New

York encountered monumental ticketing and scheduling problems. Private capitalism, still without state support, now rose to the challenge of combining the disparate lines into a system.

In 1850 Erastus Corning, president of the Albany and Schenectady Railroad and grandfather of the present mayor of Albany, began negotiating with the other nine roads about a merger. In 1853 he became the first president of the New York Central Railroad, a position he held until 1855, when it was discovered that he had been selling tracks and wheels to the Central at inflated prices. Corning was apparently interested less in developing a railroad system than in controlling a large market for his wheel and track business. New leadership took over.

The most ambitious of the early companies was the Hudson River Railroad, organized by Poughkeepsie businessmen in 1842. The backers announced that they were going to build a line along the east bank of the Hudson from New York City to Albany. John Jervis, the former laborer on the Erie Canal, was hired to design and build it.

Constructing a railroad along the river was almost as great an undertaking as digging a canal from the Hudson to Lake Erie, and the project was being financed with private capital. Hundreds of coves and inlets had to be bridged. The tides of the lower Hudson, from Manhattan to Troy, have a range of as much as four feet, and these would affect the construction. There were also the special obstacles of the Hudson Highlands, where steep granite mountains drop sharply to the river and where the water is more than a hundred feet deep.

Jervis proved himself an extraordinary administrator as well as a capable engineer. Numerous construction contracts were awarded and supervised. The land acquisition program was pushed along despite the opposition of wealthy landowners, who often demanded a private railroad station as a condition for the sale of their property.

The line opened in 1849, running from a roundhouse at 33rd Street on Manhattan's West Side to the city of Peekskill in northern Westchester County. By 1851 it was opened all the way to Albany. The alignment was the straightest in the nation and the grade was the most level. Six trains made the run. They featured first-class coaches constructed of mahogany, with velvet seats and silver plaques engraved with the company letters fastened to black enamel doors.

The boom in steamboats, city building, and railroads began to change the appearance of the Hudson. In many spots the scenic wilderness gave way to urbanization and the man-made structures one sees today. Jervis' Hudson River Railroad embankment, for example, is basically the same right of way that Penn Central trains now use.

In the midst of the transformation came the first doubting voices and the forebears of those who later opposed power plants or highways along the river. Their words were less angry than mournful, recalling, like Washington Irving in *Spanish Papers,* the "good old days, before steamboats and railroads had driven the poetry and romance out of travel." Irving described the Hudson of his childhood, before the canal—"when all the world had a tinge of fairyland. . . . We enjoyed the river then. We relished it as we did our wine, sip by sip; not as at the present gulping it down without tasting it."

The Hudson River Railroad slashed by Sunnyside, Irving's home on the river. That fact alone might have aroused his opposition. But he and other romantic writers had professional reasons as well. Irving, James Fenimore Cooper, and William Cullen Bryant—America's first men of letters—were arguing the virtues of nature as a source of artistic inspiration. European romantics also valued nature, but they preached the importance of juxtaposing a natural setting with a symbol of antiquity. The Europeans felt that a landscape containing a hillside or forest with a castle or Greek ruin helped an artist develop an appropriate sense of mystery and wonder about the past. This association of natural beauty and ancient man-made forms was vital to the European romantics of the early nineteenth century. But since American writers had no ruins to go to for inspiration, they argued that an artist could do without the buildings and concentrate on nature alone. This is how James Fenimore Cooper outlined the argument in an 1852 essay entitled "American and European Scenery Compared":

> The greater natural freedom that exists in an ordinary American landscape . . . rends the view of this country strikingly beautiful when it is of sufficient extent to conceal the want of finish in the details, which require time and long-continued labor to accomplish. . . . We conceive that the older portions of the United States offer to the eye a general outline of view that may well claim to be of even a higher cast than most of the scenery of the Old World.

To expand his point Cooper presented his tales of Leatherstocking, the unfettered man of the forest. Leatherstocking was the antithesis of civilization, a noble savage who found the spirit of God deep in the wild. "I have been a solitary man much of my time," says Leatherstocking, "if he can be called solitary, who has lived for seventy years in the very bosom of nature, and where he could at any instant open his heart to God without having to strip it of the cares and wickedness of the settlements. . . ." Earlier in 1830 William Cullen Bryant dwelled on the spiritual significance of nature to the point of paganism in his "American Landscape":

> *Foreigners who have visited our country . . . have spoken of a far spread wilderness, a look as if the new world was fresher from the hand of him who made it, the rocks and the very hillocks wearing the shape which he fashioned them . . . in short, of something which, more than any scenery to which they have become accustomed, suggested the idea of unity and immensity, and abstracting the mind from the associations of human agency, carried it up to the idea of a higher power, and to the great mystery of the origin of things.*

The American writers championed the cause of raw nature for nationalistic as well as artistic reasons. They were convinced that uniquely American art forms could be encouraged only by the originality of the landscape. "Go forth, under the open sky, and list to Nature's teachings," Bryant advised painters as well as writers. Asher Brown Durand and Thomas Cole were among the landscape artists who did. Their pictures of the Catskill and highlands regions of the Hudson stress lush natural scenes rather than structures and seldom contain people. The Hudson River School was America's first distinctive break with European artists, and the underlying philosophy was expressed by Cole in a letter to Durand. "In landscapes," he wrote his colleague in 1832, "there is a greater variety of objects, textures, phenomena, to imitate. It has expression, also, not of passion to be sure, but of sentiment, whether it be tranquil or spirit-stirring."

Eventually the Americans won their artistic battle with the Europeans, many of whom came over to the side of nature by following Cole and Bryant into the woods. But the artists and writers had no immediate impact on their fellow Americans, who were determined, also for nationalistic reasons, to build even more canals and railroads. No interprofessional debates, protests, or litigation arose from the suddenly perceived aesthetic virtues of nature. Yet though it was business as usual, a fundamental conflict in American values was born and expressed for the first time.

The pastoral impulse of Bryant, Irving, and Cooper had a great impact on American literature. Emerson, Melville, Hemingway, Frost, and Faulkner were to rely heavily on ocean, forest, and wilderness settings. Professor Leo Marx of Amherst College argues that the present ecology movement actually springs from American writing. The view that man is but one part of a sensitive, interdependent natural system is what Bryant, Irving, and Cooper were saying all along.

More than a hundred years later, in the defense of Storm King Mountain, Vincent Skully, Jr., of Yale University sounded less like a contemporary observer than a Hudson River romantic when he described the mountain to the FPC hearing examiner:

> *It rises like a brown bear out of the water, a dome of living granite, swelling with animal power. It is not picturesque in the softer sense of the word, but awesome, a primitive embodiment of the energies of the earth. It*

THE CANAL

makes the character of wild nature visible in monumental form. . . .

The examiner was not attuned to those sentiments; nor was Con Edison, which supported the values represented earlier by the builders of the Erie Canal.

The canal had demonstrated man's superiority over nature and had opened the frontier. It bore a uniquely American stamp, and gave rise to democracy along what had been the most auto-cratic river in the United States. But most important, it had a major impact on the American mind. A massive engineering project meant progress and confidence in the future. If the Erie Canal could be built, anything was possible.

THE COMPANY

Con Edison is a major corporation and the largest private utility in the nation. Con Edison sells the gas, steam, and electricity that New York City needs to operate and to grow. Con Edison produces urban energy.

About 20,000 people work for Con Edison, and their experience is unique in that they never really escape their jobs. Rather they are reminded of them through mundane experiences that most of us take for granted, such as watching television, seeing a spotlight on a stage, or just making some toast.

Late in the afternoon of November 9, 1965, the chief engi-

neer at Con Edison was descending into the Lexington Avenue
Subway at 14th Street when suddenly the lights went out. In
the midst of the confusion he groped his way back up the stairs;
seeing the darkened city all around him, he became the first
New Yorker on the street to know that he would be very late
getting home that night. He located a policeman from whom he
asked assistance in getting to Con Edison's control center near
Lincoln Center. He explained that he might be able to get the
lights on again, but the patrolman wouldn't believe him. So the
engineer, like the rest of New York City's inhabitants, stumbled
in the darkness of the great November blackout.

Con Edison's origins are tied to the history of the Hudson
River following the opening of the Erie Canal. Between 1825
and the Civil War villages became cities, sailors became entrepreneurs, tenants became property owners, and merchants began
to run railroads. But the local railroads, proud products of a free
market, did not always connect. The steamboat races, exemplify-
ing the spirit of open competition, were also killing or otherwise
inconveniencing passengers. With the exception of the Erie
Canal, the valley had few ties with the rest of the nation.

Beginning in the middle of the nineteenth century the
Hudson Valley produced a new breed of entrepreneurs, the so-
called robber barons, who established order and control over
business. Some of the robber barons bought out the independent
boat lines and merged them. Others acquired the independent
railroads and transformed them into regional, then national systems. Still others acquired small banks, insurance companies,
and utilities and merged them into citywide or statewide corporations.

This strangulation of free enterprise provoked the outrage

of at least one generation of writers, journalists, and public officials. Were the robber barons an economic cancer or merely the instruments of self-correction produced by a runaway economy? Whatever their function, they performed it colorfully. They also created Con Edison.

Two early Hudson River robber barons who emerged during the postcanal period were Daniel Drew and Cornelius Vanderbilt. Drew began as a drover in the Hudson Highlands, where he gathered cattle from Putnam County farms and led them to the meat markets of Manhattan's Third Avenue. Drew kept his herds dry until they arrived a block away from the market, where they were encouraged to drink all the water they could hold, thereby increasing their weight and Drew's profits. From this practice came the expression "watered stock." Drew's profits from watered stock were invested in the Bull's Head Tavern. He used his gains from the tavern to buy steamships. Drew was no seaman; he simply knew how to buy other people's boats at low prices. He welded his purchases into the People's Line, which by the middle of the nineteenth century controlled most of the Hudson River steamboat traffic.

Vanderbilt was a sailor. As a young man he piloted sailboat ferries to New York from Staten Island, where he was born and now rests in a million-dollar crypt overlooking New York Harbor. Vanderbilt bought a steamship and then gradually acquired those his competitors. The "Commodore," as he was called, was the most ruthless businessman on the river. He often sabotaged his competitors, and there is some evidence to suggest that he even may have murdered one or two. A mild example of the Commodore's style was a race between one of his ships and a steamer called the *Oregon* in 1847 on a run

THE COMPANY

from New York City to Croton-on-Hudson and back again. When the *Oregon* began taking the lead, the Commodore's boat veered into its stern, destroying a portion of the paddle wheel.

Drew and Vanderbilt were adversaries in the early days of their shipping careers. Later they became distrustful allies and then bitter enemies in the takeover of the railroads.

Their interest in trains began when the Hudson River Railroad opened its line to Albany in 1851. The Hudson road was a direct and open challenge to the steamers. The trains ran right along the river, moved much faster than the steamers, and operated during the winter, when the river was frozen. There were three other major railroads in the Hudson Valley: the New York Central, with tracks from Albany to Buffalo; the Erie, with a line from Piermont-on-Hudson across the rugged southern tier of New York State to Dunkirk on Lake Erie; and the Harlem River Railroad, with tracks between New York City and Chatham, New York. Two of these railroad companies were financially troubled: the Erie and the Harlem River. Those were the lines that Drew and Vanderbilt grabbed first.

Vanderbilt acquired majority interest in the Harlem River Railroad in 1857. His method was direct. Harlem stock was cheap and the Commodore quietly purchased all that he could get. The Commodore's interest in the Harlem line was intended to frighten the Poughkeepsie backers of the Hudson River Railroad. He announced that he was going to improve the Harlem line and make it competitive with the Hudson for freight and passenger business between New York and Albany. The effect of his challenge was a sudden reduction in the value of Hudson River Railroad stock, which the Commodore also bought on the sly. By 1865 he owned a majority of the Hudson River Railroad stock and controlled all the major north-south rail lines on the east bank of the Hudson.

Drew, in the meantime, was concentrating on the west bank. In 1851 he loaned $1.5 million to the Erie Railroad on the condition that he would acquire control of the railroad if the loan was not repaid. In 1858 he became the Erie's chief executive officer. Financial observers and the directors of the New York Central—the principal competitor of the Erie—wondered what Drew had in mind. In 1858 he launched a rate war with the Central over the shipment of goods from the Hudson Valley to Lake Erie. Central stock tumbled in value.

Drew and Vanderbilt then combined in a pincers movement. While Drew bombarded the Central's rates, the Commodore raised the charges for Central passengers and freight transferring at Albany for the trip south to New York City on the Hudson River Railroad. The directors of the Central were ambushed. Their principal competitor and the rail and shipping links from its Albany terminus to New York City were under the control of two belligerents. In 1865 the Commodore rushed in for the kill and acquired the Central, which he merged with his Hudson River Railroad. The stage was then set for a dramatic showdown between the two barons for control of all the major rail lines in the Hudson Valley.

By 1867 Vanderbilt had acquired 20 percent of the Erie's stock and was rocking Wall Street as he sought majority control. Drew fortified himself with two younger men: Jay Gould and Jim Fisk. Gould was a Catskill farm boy whose name, financial skill, and "Jewish cast of face" caused the Commodore to wonder aloud whether he was dealing with a fellow Christian gentleman. Gould married into some wealth, then gained his financial reputation as a railroad scavenger. He purchased small, bankrupt lines, made some marginal improvements in their operation, then pretended that he was going to give some competitive railroad company, usually a larger one, a race for customers. His technique was basically a smaller version of the Commodore's tactics against the Hudson River Railroad, except that Gould used competition to sell rather than to acquire. In the beginning of his career Gould usually ended up selling his small railroad companies for their nuisance value, which was greater in dollars than what Gould had paid for them in the first place. Fisk too was a clever manipulator. He was born in poverty and had honed his business skills as a dispenser of homemade medicines which he sold from a wagon along the backroads of the Lake Champlain area.

Fisk, Gould, and Drew, the three principal executives of the Erie, counterattacked the Commodore by flooding the market with watered Erie stock. When the Commodore realized he was purchasing worthless paper, he turned to William M. ("Boss") Tweed, the New York political leader, who for a price persuaded a judge to enjoin the Erie leaders from issuing any more stock. A sheriff's party was dispatched to arrest the trio in the spring of 1868.

Fisk, Gould, and Drew also had friends in high places. When they learned that they were about to be arrested, they emptied the safe at Erie headquarters on Water Street in Manhattan and, accompanied by sixty guards, made their way to the Hudson, where they boarded a flotilla of boats and crossed to Jersey City. Local police surrounded the Taylor House, where they were staying, to beat off a threatened attack by thugs hired by the Commodore. Inside, the three men held press conferences. Gould told reporters that the Erie was the bulwark of free enterprise and that he and his colleagues were engaged in a fight of principle against the greed of Vanderbilt. Drew took matters less seriously. He quipped that the Erie was merely following Horace Greeley's advice and had moved west for a while. Fisk, locked in a room with his mistress, seldom made statements to the press.

Some weeks later Vanderbilt offered to negotiate. A settlement was arranged on the condition that Vanderbilt would be repaid for his investment in worthless stock and that the Erie would be left alone. Drew and Fisk died not long after, and Gould became the head of the Erie.

The adventurous styles of Vanderbilt, Drew, and Gould produced transportation systems, but they also unsettled the economy. Stock manipulations and the use of thugs, sabotage, and purchased court orders were crude methods of building railroads and settling financial disagreements. They were hardly an inducement to investment either.

The Civil War severely drained the American economy. European credit became a critical necessity in the postwar years, but the Dutch and British investors were appalled by the crudeness of the American capitalists, just as they had been dismayed by the unskilled canal builders earlier in the century. The situation called for someone to take charge, clean things up, and curb the system of its competitive excesses.

J. Pierpont Morgan, the new housekeeper of American capitalism, was also the midwife for the Consolidated Gas Company, the predecessor of Con Edison. Like DeWitt Clinton, a prototype of contemporary politicians, Morgan was an early model for contemporary corporate executives. He was quite different from the earlier robber barons. Born of the middle class, he had attended college and had a secure upbringing. Unlike Vanderbilt, who ran his operations from a cigar box, Morgan relied on lawyers and accountants. He was an organization man.

Some of the distinctiveness of Morgan's style is evident in his Hudson River retreat, Cragston, located several miles south of Storm King Mountain in Highland Falls. The Hudson mansions of Gould and Vanderbilt are European imitations. Lyndhurst, the Gould mansion in Irvington, is a neo-Gothic monstrosity, a bit frightening, like its owner. The Vanderbilt mansion in Hyde Park is American Versailles, complete with gold-leafed ceilings, tapestries, and ornate furnishings either inspired by or actually ripped from European villas.

Morgan's home was built in a native Victorian style, with carefully hewn timbers, gently curving cornices, and gingerbread ornamentation. Cragston is a large-scale version of a typical Hudson River house of the late nineteenth century. While other Hudson mansions were showpieces, Cragston was a home and the Morgans had a good time there. The children had ponies and carriages; they took walks in the woods and enjoyed picnics and games on the lawn. The Cragston estate typifies some of the personal and business values that Morgan held dear. In the summer of 1883 he ordered his children to keep their carriages and ponies in the barn and to stay away from the eastern side of the estate, which sloped toward the Hudson. The reason for his order was that a new railroad line, the West Shore, was being constructed through Highland Falls north to Storm King Mountain and Cornwall. Morgan was upset. His tranquility was ruined by the rock blasting, his view hindered by mounds of raw dirt, and his family's security, he feared, threatened by hundreds of unruly-looking laborers.

The new railroad line was also an example of thoughtless,

destructive, and unnecessary competition, which Morgan was determined to stamp out. The West Shore line was secretly being financed by the Pennsylvania Railroad as payment in kind for the New York Central's invasion into Pennsylvania. Before his death in 1877, Commodore Vanderbilt authorized the construction of a new Central line across Pennsylvania to Pittsburgh. The Pennsylvania Railroad retaliated with the West Shore line, an open challenge to the Central's route along the east bank of the Hudson.

Despite Morgan's profound annoyance and his appointment in 1882 to the Central board, he did nothing to stop the West Shore line until its trains were actually in service in 1886. Only after its real-dollar as opposed to nuisance value was established did Morgan intervene as mediator, a role that he was performing in other corporate struggles. He summoned the executives of the two railroads to his yacht, the *Corsair,* for a cruise up the Hudson. During the trip he persuaded the Pennsylvania's leaders to sell the West Shore line to the Central in return for the Central's agreement to abandon its plans for a new Pittsburgh line.

The West Shore line remained in service because it made money. Morgan thus joined the ranks of other Hudson River estate owners who had trains crossing near or through their property. Neither Morgan nor the others seemed to mind the traffic as much as Washington Irving did.

The gas utilities of New York were a prime attraction for the robber barons. The utilities enjoyed monopoly positions, their profits were high, and their growth prospects were very good. The possibilities for empire building were great, but so was the likelihood of destructive competition among warring investors. Morgan was determined that the utilities would not be exposed to the same foolish struggles as the railroads.

Like the railroads, the utilities began as small independent businesses. In 1823 a special aldermanic committee in New York City made the historic judgment that private enterprise, rather than a municipal corporation, would introduce gas lighting to the city. Several of the committee's members later became directors of the four original gas companies in Manhattan. The decision in favor of private gas production and distribution prompted a frantic rush to obtain franchises, not unlike the current race among cable television companies.

The only restrictions placed on the new utilities were that they remain in their assigned districts and that they use cast iron mains. The requirement for iron pipe resulted from the city's experience with its first private utility, the Manhattan Water Company, headed by Aaron Burr, which used hollow logs as mains. The logs rotted quickly, disrupting the water supply and turning the streets of New York to mud.

By 1836 the first gas utility, the New York Gas Company, had installed its iron mains and was delivering gas to homes and businesses in a district that ran from the southern tip of Manhattan north to Canal Street. Then came the Manhattan Gas Company in the area between Canal Street and what is now the southern edge of midtown Manhattan. The Metropolitan Gas Company serviced the present midtown area, and the Harlem Gas Company, the last to obtain a franchise, was given the farmland of upper Manhattan.

The new companies were not very popular. Customers complained of overcharging, and an organization called the Gas Consumers Association attacked the legality of the franchises.

The association also criticized the utilities' monopoly position and demanded an official investigation into their rate structures. A city investigation was undertaken in 1851, but the investigators, some of whom were gas company directors, dismissed the association's charges. The introduction of gas meters around this time furthered the public relations problems. Customers, who preferred a flat monthly fee, were suspicious of the machines, and their anxieties sparked a new business in the city: the sale of dogs trained to bite the meter readers.

The most severe complaints about the gas companies came from those who lived in the vicinity of the gas works. The companies made gas by reducing coal to coke, a process that produces hydrogen sulphide and ammonia gas as by-products. The smell of that combination could "knock down a horse and bowl over men," according to an 1842 comment from an assistant engineer at one of the Manhattan Gas Company's plants. To get rid of the odor before distribution, the gas was passed through lime water. The result, called "blue billy," was stored in the plant, then carted for dumping to the nearest waterway. But the aroma of rotten eggs and ammonia persisted in the plants.

The effect was crippling on nearby neighborhoods. Complaints from people living near the Metropolitan Gas Company's 42nd Street plant were so bitter that the New York City Board of Health threatened to close down the gas works. Metropolitan officers asked the health inspectors to check the bloated corpses of several dead horses in a lot adjacent to the plant. Perhaps, they said, the corpses were to blame. The horses were removed, but the aroma remained, so the Metropolitan officials mounted a new defense. The smell of their plant might be terrible, they admitted, but it was a sure cure for whooping cough.

To bolster the claim they made the plant available, as a community service, to coughing children from all over the city. Strangely enough, the treatment worked and the Board of Health allowed the plant to remain in operation.

The appalling smells of the gas works made it difficult to find or keep workers. The companies turned to immigrant labor for help. The largest group of newly arrived Europeans in the middle of the nineteenth century was the Irish, and they soon dominated the ranks of the gas companies below the managerial level. Executive employees were usually native WASPs. The early preponderance of laborers from Ireland led to the enduring belief that the New York utilities hired only the Irish. It also created some immediate problems. The Manhattan Gas Company was almost forced to close during the Civil War as its employees began quitting in droves to join the 69th Irish Regiment. To stop the exodus, the Manhattan formed its own Irish fighting unit, the 37th Regiment, which was composed of gas workers and was commanded by the company president, Charles Roome. To indulge his employees' apparent appetite for combat Roome led them to Carlisle, Pennsylvania, for a one-day battle, after which they returned to the city to operate and guard the gas works.

Many of the executives and directors of the gas companies were shrewd politicians. This skill was demanded of them because the companies depended on good will from city hall. The companies therefore competed with one another to persuade city officials to serve on their boards. The Manhattan Gas Company won the race in 1862, when the directors convinced the mayor of New York, George Opdyke, to serve on the board. Opdyke's political foes charged that the mayor made money at the public's expense during his dual service. Opdyke sued one of his accusers but could not get a jury to agree that he had been libeled.

All the utilities courted Boss Tweed during his brief but remarkable political reign in the post-Civil War years. Tweed had resolved several disputes between the city and two of the utilities over alleged overcharges for street fixtures and gas rates. The bills were paid promptly. In return the directors of the gas companies came to Tweed's defense in 1869 when *The New York Times* and *Harper's Weekly* attacked him for squandering city funds. Moses Taylor of the Manhattan Gas Company and Jacob Astor of the New York Gas Company were among a group of prominent businessmen who claimed that the city's funds were in order. They also proposed that rather than try to imprison Tweed, the public should show its gratitude for his good works by erecting a statue in his honor in New York Harbor.

The utilities' alliance with Tweed made them the targets of zealous reformers who took over the city after Tweed's emergency exit to Spain. The main punishment was a city ordinance, passed in 1872, permitting any company with enough money to enter the gas business. The monopoly on gas was over. Four new companies were formed in Manhattan. Others started in the outlying boroughs. The new Manhattan entries invaded the territory of the original gas companies. They also introduced cheaper, cleaner gas. The New York Mutual Company used naphtha instead of coal as a base. The Equitable Gas Company sold "water gas," which was made by passing steam over hot coals.

Under the competitive and technological assault the original gas companies were forced to lower costs, which required more efficient production. Discarded coke, ammonia water, and tar—the by-products of gas production—were saved and marketed. By 1875 the gas business seemed to be a model of free competition, and customers were the main beneficiaries, just as they had been for a brief time when the Harlem River Railroad challenged the Hudson River Railroad and the Erie started a rate war with the New York Central. But the real cause for competition in all cases was the robber barons' manipulation of market forces in order to gain control of the gas companies. Commodore Vanderbilt and his son William were the principal backers of the new Equitable Gas Company. William Rockefeller, the brother of John D. Rockefeller, was the main investor in the Knickerbocker Gas Light Company, another new firm. With the help of James Stillman, whose National City Bank held most of the family money, Rockefeller used the Knickerbocker Company as a wedge to take over others. Morgan moved in as a major investor in the Municipal Gas Light Company, another new firm from which he hoped to exert a moderating influence against the free-for-all combat among the barons that seemed bound to break out.

The potential for chaos was heightened by the introduction of electricity as a technological rival to gas. The opening of the Brooklyn Bridge in 1883 aroused popular interest in electricity. Among the remarkable features of the new bridge were its carbon arc lamps, which lit the sky above and the water below. The bridge lights and some earlier electric street lamps installed along Broadway were the products of new, fledgling electric arc companies.

Morgan was several steps ahead of everyone in appreciating the financial as well as technological implications of electric lighting. If the gas companies fought with one another while being invaded by the electric companies, the utility business would be in a shambles. There was time for alternative arrangements. Electric lighting needed to improve technically before it could compete for the lucrative indoor market. The carbon arc lamps were extremely bright and noisy, and they burned out quickly. They were also hooked in series. If one blew out, the entire system darkened. Morgan figured that if he could control the necessary technological improvements, he would have the wedge he needed to drive out harmful competition.

In 1878, when the new electric street light companies began operations, Morgan induced several financiers to join with him in backing the work of Thomas Edison, who was devising an entirely new system of interior electric lighting in his Menlo Park, New Jersey, laboratory. Morgan had to be very persuasive because backing Edison was risky business. Edison was regarded by many as a mad scientist—the "Wizard of Menlo Park" was how one newspaper described him. But Morgan prevailed. He and his friends institutionalized the wizard. They set up a research corporation, the Edison Electric Light Company, which paid for Edison's laboratory, gave him and his associates decent salaries, and held the patents to his inventions.

Edison applied existing research and improved other people's inventions in developing a new system of electric lighting. He devised a new filament for incandescent bulbs so that they would burn longer and brighter. He adapted the new lamps to a multiple-arc system, in which each lamp burned independently of the others. He improved Faraday's dynamo, the powerhouse of his new system, and when he put it all together he had a more flexible and economical system of electric lighting, for indoor as well as outdoor use, than the system being used by the street light companies.

Edison used Morgan's mansion on Madison Avenue as a testing ground. Despite the protests of neighbors, who complained that the noise kept them awake and that the smoke tarnished their silverware, Morgan was delighted by all the gadgets. A dynamo had been placed in his yard. Edison had strung wires through the mansion's gas conduits and inserted the lamps in the gas fixtures. After some minor mishaps, including short circuits and a brief fire, Morgan and his friends judged the Edison system workable and ready for marketing. The research company sold its first franchise to the Edison Electric Illuminating Company in 1880, with Edison overseeing the installation of its dynamo and wires in lower Manhattan along Pearl Street.

Even at this crude stage of electrical production and distribution, Edison was remarkably sensitive to the environmental problems of power production. The dynamo for the Edison Electric Illuminating Company was placed in a rundown section of the neighborhood, and the transmission lines were buried. The maze of overhead telegraph wires in Manhattan was so great that in 1888 the Common Council ordered all utility companies to follow Edison's lead.

While Edison installed his new service, Morgan was meeting with the investors of the various gas utilities, pointing out the dangers of their competitive ways. The new Edison system would revolutionize the utility business, he predicted. The profit outlook was bright, Morgan stressed, and everyone would make money, but only if the companies began cooperating. Some of the owners, like William Vanderbilt, did whatever Morgan advised. Others, like William Rockefeller and James Stillman, were less easily persuaded but were impressed by his logic as well as his control over the promising Edison system. On November 4, 1884, Morgan's behind-the-scenes efforts paid off with the formation of the Consolidated Gas Company with which most of the independent gas utilities merged and which thereupon controlled almost half of all the gas production and distribution facilities in the city. The announcement stunned consumer organizations whose leaders thought that the 1872 ordinance establishing open competition in the utility business meant an end to gas monopolies. But now, due to the robber barons, the old district monopolies had been replaced by a city-wide monopoly. The cries of protest from consumer groups and the press had no effect. Following the 1884 consolidation, the new gas company gradually acquired all the remaining independent companies.

While public attention was riveted on the new colossus, with its few defenders arguing that one large gas producer would still be in technological competition with the electric companies, Morgan, Vanderbilt, Stillman, and Rockefeller were organizing a still greater financial coup, the acquisition of the electric companies by the new Consolidated Gas Company. This was made possible by the demonstrated superiority of the Edison system over other lighting systems and its immediate adaptability to the indoor market. Through their ownership of the Edison Electric Light Company, Morgan and his partners controlled the patent for the Edison system and therefore the distribution of franchises. Investors in the new Edison companies were financial allies. Beginning in 1898 the Edison lighting companies began affiliating with Consolidated Gas. By 1900 Consolidated Gas

THE COMPANY

had become an enormous holding company for virtually all of the gas and electric utilities of New York City. The robber barons had closed out the nineteenth century with one of their more formidable accomplishments.

POWER

By the beginning of the twentieth century the moguls of shipping, railroads, and the utilities realized that there were no more financial worlds to conquer; and because they were growing old, they were anxious to leave behind some personal mementos in addition to their institutional triumphs. The Hudson Valley today has many examples of the directions they followed in their twilight years.

Lyndhurst, the Gould estate in Irvington, introduces their late-blooming interest in beauty. On the grounds of Lyndhurst are the remnants of a large rose garden and the skeleton of an immense greenhouse as large as a railroad station. Gould became a fanatical gardener toward the end of his life, and he acquired and cultivated plants with the same fury that he had previously taken over companies.

In 1885 James Stillman, who as president of the National City Bank was a prime organizer of the Consolidated Gas Company, purchased a large section of Storm King Mountain for the purpose of transforming it into a dramatic site for a colony of country homes for his family and friends. The layout was to have been similar to but grander than that of Tuxedo Park, a resort for the upper classes of New York which had recently been established in the hills of Orange County, southwest of Storm King, by Pierre Lorillard, owner of the tobacco company. Lorillard refused to admit Stillman to Tuxedo Park because he was regarded as *nouveau riche.* Stillman was thus deprived of enjoying Tuxedo Park's three lakes, its bridle paths, and its tennis courts, not to mention participating in the compound's annual autumn ball which was regarded as the formal opening of the winter social season in New York. Stillman, much annoyed, decided to build something nicer on Storm King Mountain. His interest in the mountain later provided a note of irony, since by staking a claim on Storm King in 1963 Con Edison was invading the hideaway of one of its founders. Stillman died before his development plans bore fruit. In 1928 his heirs gave a portion of his holdings, called the Black Rock Forest, to Harvard University. The mountain property was turned over to the Palisades Park Commission.

The robber barons and other wealthy river families helped create the Palisades Park Commission in 1900 for the acquisition and protection of choice river land. Some of the financial titans set aside bitter business quarrels to aid the commission in its work. Gould, Harriman, Rockefeller, and Morgan were among the largest contributors to the purchase of the Palisade Cliffs in northern New Jersey and southern New York on the west bank of the Hudson. The Palisades campaign was organized by George Perkins, president of the New York Metropolitan Life Insurance Company, who quit his job to become the first chief executive of the commission.

The barons also threw their support behind the Adirondack Forest Preserve, a wilderness area in northern New York State where the Hudson River begins. An 1895 amendment to the state constitution protected the Adirondacks from the ravages wrought by lumbermen and hotel developers. It also assured the continuing serenity of the numerous Adirondack "camps" such as the 112,000-acre retreat, including a railroad station, owned by William Vanderbilt's son-in-law, and J. P. Morgan's spread on Tupper Lake.

The numerous land and park gifts of wealthy river families also left a mark on the conservation movement in the valley. The barons made conservation a practical real estate proposition by acquiring unspoiled tracts of land, such as the Palisades, for the purpose of protecting them from tawdry commercial interests. The barons also contributed to the city-beautiful movement in New York. In the nineteenth century Frederick Law Olmstead had been hired to create Central and Prospect parks. The parks added a touch of beauty to New York. They also made handsome sites for the new museums of the city, one of whose purposes was to provide shelter for the barons' burgeoning art collections. The early trustees of the Metropolitan Museum, as well as its original founders, included many men serving on the board of the Consolidated Gas Company or its affiliates. The

Metropolitan's unusually large collection of armor is explained by J. P. Morgan's enthusiasm as a collector. Morgan was a prime backer of the Metropolitan.

The distribution and shelter of the barons' art collections usually became the responsibility of the heirs, some of whom, such as John D. Rockefeller, Jr., handled the assignment with sensitivity. He had the good sense to base his museum decisions on the advice of experts. He also refined the practice of giving away money as well as art. The outstanding Rockefeller contribution to the Hudson Valley is the Cloisters and the surrounding Fort Tryon Park, located just north of the George Washington Bridge on the New York City side of the river. The Cloisters contains the Metropolitan's medieval collection, virtually all of which was either contributed or paid for by Rockefeller. He also gave the sixty-acre park to New York City. The Cloisters was developed during the construction of the George Washington Bridge and the Henry Hudson Parkway, which begins at the New York side of the bridge and winds northward above the river beneath the Cloisters. Rockefeller worked with the Port of New York Authority as well as with New York City Parks Commissioner Robert Moses on the projects. He bought all the land on the Palisades side of the bridge in view of the museum to prevent its commercial development. The coordination of the various elements of the program—the open space, bridge, parkway, and museum—represented a major administrative challenge. By taking it on, Rockefeller produced excellent examples of good urban planning and the wonders that money can accomplish.

Of all the structures in the Hudson Valley that are monuments to the robber barons none is more symbolic than Grand Central Station, which was opened by Vanderbilt's New York

Central Railroad at the beginning of the twentieth century. In his appraisal of nineteenth-century buildings, architectural historian Carl Condit ranks Grand Central as "the greatest work of building and civic art ever undertaken by a railroad company." Despite its location in midtown Manhattan, at least a mile from the river, Grand Central Station is a testimony to nineteenth-century Hudson River history. No winds from the north beat down on this building, with its artificial sky painted on a 125-foot-high ceiling. It is an entranceway to Manhattan that is fit for an emperor. Passengers wishing to travel up the Hudson proceed down a ramp to board a train that takes them beneath Park Avenue for forty-four blocks, up along the path of the old Harlem River Railroad, and northwest along the Harlem River to the Hudson. The best of the trains was the Twentieth Century Limited, now defunct, which began its evening run to Chicago in 1902. It offered a sunset dinner in the Hudson Highlands following champagne cocktails served as the train sped past the home of Washington Irving.

The elegant days of railroading are gone now. The old adversary empires, the New York Central and the Pennsylvania, have merged and fallen into bankruptcy. On the south side of Grand Central Station stands a poignant example of decline. It is a seldom noticed statue of Commodore Vanderbilt located at the end of the ramp leading north from Park Avenue to the upper level of the station. The Commodore's cloak is covered in soot, his bald head coated by pigeon droppings; his expression, as he peers southward through the smog of Park Avenue, is one of puzzlement. He seems now to be a more distant figure of history than a man who along with a few others made things happen in the Hudson Valley less than a hundred years ago.

While the robber barons sought immortality in statues, monuments, cliffs, and museums at the opening of the twentieth century, the public was just beginning to appreciate the enormity of their economic power. In addition to controlling utilities and railroads, critics charged, they deliberately created depressions and inflationary cycles just to suit the needs of their investment portfolios. Earnest public officials, reacting to the popular demand for protection and revenge, set out to destroy the citadels of financial power. One of the chief targets was the Consolidated Gas Company, or "the gas trust" as it came to be called in the pre-World War I era of muckraking journalism.

The trustees of the Consolidated Gas Company simply ignored or perhaps misgauged the depth of the public protest that accompanied announcement of the formation of the gas and electric company in 1900. In 1904 they blithely decreed new increases in gas and electricity rates while declaring a 10 percent dividend to the stockholders. The combined rate hike and dividend sparked new demands for investigation, but this time they came from a wider group than the company's traditional enemies, consumer organizations and press critics. The mayor of New York, George B. McClellan, expressed outrage. The City Club and Merchants Association also joined the attack.

Even the state legislature, not normally willing to take on large New York companies, rumbled with discontent over Consolidated's apparent greed. State Senator Frederick Stevens, a moderate and influential lawmaker, was elected chairman of a special joint investigating committee. Suddenly the trustees and executives of Consolidated found themselves, and their records, subpoenaed by Stevens' committee.

Their chief interrogator was the committee counsel, a

young and unknown lawyer named Charles Evans Hughes. After three weeks of hearings, Hughes was a celebrity. He revealed that Consolidated Gas was charging most of its gas customers three times more than the actual operating and capital costs of gas production. The city government's rates were four times greater than those of large companies. The bookkeeping was a mystery. The controversial dividend, for example, was apparently based on the market value of company stock at the time rather than on a percentage of annual company profits. A total of $8 million had been distributed in dividend checks, a healthy sum in those days; and it was apparently nothing more than a pleasant gesture to the stockholders. Hughes also uncovered various interlocking directorships between the gas company and the railroad, aluminum, insurance, and electrical-manufacturing industries. New York Life, National City Bank, General Electric, the Aluminum Company of America, New York Central, and the Equitable Society were among the firms with investments and director representatives in the Consolidated Gas Company, which Hughes portrayed as a huge conspiracy.

As the first outsider to take an intensive look at the company, Hughes was in an excellent position to determine what should be done. His most important recommendation was that the company be placed under public regulation rather than broken up in order to restore competition. The New York State Public Service Commission undertook the job in 1907, which was also Hughes' first year as Governor of the state. His 1904 performance was so sensational that he was handed the Republican gubernatorial nomination and went on to defeat William Randolph Hearst in the 1906 election. Another of Hughes' recommendations was the imposition of fixed rates of 80 cents per thousand cubic feet for gas and 10 cents per kilowatt hour for electricity. Consolidated Gas fought the rate freeze until 1923, when the freeze was overruled by the U.S. Supreme Court.

Hughes' inquiry, recommendations, and sanctions were directed primarily at the trustees and financiers of the Consolidated Gas Company. His crusade overlooked the engineers and technicians, and that proved to be a serious, if understandable, error. The robber barons' role in the company had diminished considerably by the beginning of the twentieth century—they were, after all, plucking roses and planning museums by the time of Hughes' investigation. The financiers had organized Consolidated Gas for profit and were happy now merely to collect their dividend checks. But as a force within the company they were rapidly being replaced by a new breed of engineer managers whose technological innovations and bureaucratic methods kept the company under tight centralized control in the twentieth century.

By the second decade of the century the primary markets for gas and electricity had been allotted. Electricity had proven its superiority as a lighting source, and the Edison system was the clear winner in competition with the arc lights. The original street lamp companies went broke or were merged into Consolidated Gas. Gas came to be used primarily for ovens and furnaces.

The energy sources controlled by the Consolidated Gas Company vastly changed the habits and appearance of New York City. Nighttime factory shifts, made possible by artificial light, became an established feature of the job market. Artificial light also released engineers and architects from the traditional burden of having to locate and design buildings for maximum exposure to sunlight. Buildings were packed in tightly. Quaint rural sections of the city gave way to dense urban development. The advent of motor-operated elevators made possible the construction of buildings to heights never dreamed of in the nineteenth century, when stairs and horse-driven pullies were the common methods of getting people and materials above the ground floor. Business executives who once looked out onto streets now gazed down on a city. Consolidated Gas was not just another business in New York. By supplying the needed energy, the company quite literally ran New York.

The city's increasing dependence on Consolidated Gas helped the company to expand, but the expansion was made possible by and in turn was completely dependent on engineers. The early Edison system was suited only to small, independent utility systems. Edison envisioned decentralized neighborhood power stations. His early dynamos generated low-tension direct current and the transmission lines lost voltage "pressure" if they were extended more than half a mile from the dynamo. No one knew how to tie the independent systems together. In 1900 there were 296 separate electrical generating and distribution systems serving New York.

During the first decade of the twentieth century, while the Hughes investigation was under way, the Consolidated Gas engineers devised large steam turbines, high-tension transmission lines, transformers, and rotary converters, making it possible to generate high-tension alternating current and to transmit it for as much as ten miles to substations which stepped down the current for use in homes and businesses. The equipment improvements meant economies of scale and compelled the smaller companies to affiliate. A single new turbine could replace twenty to thirty dynamos. The larger generators also required riverside lo-cations where large quantities of cooling water could be tapped. The improvements continued at a phenomenal rate. By 1920 some of the newer transmission lines and auxiliary equipment could efficiently convey electricity up to 200 miles away from a power source. This meant that citywide, regional systems were not only possible but economically desirable. The innovations also led to the use of distant hydroelectric power plants for urban energy needs. These engineering improvements created brand-new political issues such as how the larger electrical sys-tems should be set up and whether hydroelectric sites should be developed publicly or privately. Hughes and his trust busters, preoccupied with robber barons and dividend checks, missed those issues completely. They did not go unnoticed, however, within the hierarchy of Consolidated Gas.

The reaction of the company to the Hughes investigation, aside from cries of foul, was a reorganization of top manage-ment. The most important change was the installation of a new president, George B. Courtelyou, in 1909. This choice signified the trustees' awareness that they needed a man who could pave the way politically for citywide and statewide power distribution as well as for the private development of hydroelectric sites. Courtelyou was no company-bred engineer. The trustees brought him to New York from Washington, where he was Theodore Roosevelt's Postmaster General and had previously served as a secretary to President William McKinley and as an administra-tive aide to President Grover Cleveland. Courtelyou was a well-connected and influential politician. During the insurance com-pany investigations of 1906, also led by Hughes, Courtelyou was identified as the recipient for the national Republican party of large cash contributions from New York Life, Equitable Life, and Mutual Life. Several Consolidated Gas trustees also served as directors or drew fees from the insurance companies, so Courtelyou's political abilities were well known to them.

The official company history describes Courtelyou's first ten years as a "period of adversity," mainly because of a 1910 court order requiring the company to refund $10 million to its overcharged customers. The refund plus the rate freeze created some cash-flow problems during the home-front austerity of World War I, but the company's fortunes rebounded during the prosperous 1920s as Courtelyou demonstrated his political skills.

Among his numerous political allies in Albany was William Prendergast, a prominent fellow Republican and chairman of the Public Service Commission. Prendergast established the commission's early reputation as a lackluster and ineffective guardian of consumer interests. Another Courtelyou ally was Republican state chairman and House Speaker Edmund McHold. The McHold Storage Law authorized the lease, for reasonable terms, of hydroelectric sites on state rivers and at the time was cited by national populist leaders, such as Senators Ralph Norris and Robert La Follette, as an example of the control that the nation's private utilities held over state legislatures. Another Courtelyou associate was Warren Thayer, who helped rally support in the Senate for private power development, for which he was paid a regular retainer.

Alfred E. Smith was the first New York Governor to challenge the political influence of the utilities. In 1922, one month before Smith was to take office, the lame duck administration of Governor Nathan Miller was about to award leasing rights to ALCOA for the hydroelectric development of the St. Lawrence River. The lease was supported by Consolidated Gas and other state utilities. Smith dispatched a telegram to Governor Miller, along with copies to the press, demanding that the controversial lease be withheld. It was.

Smith ran for Governor on a platform promising public power development as a means of holding down electric bills. Smith felt that it was wrong for private enterprise to exploit public resources and make large profits in the bargain. Smith knew nothing about the new technology of power production but merely sensed that hydroelectric power, for instance, could mean lower rates, the issue that interested him the most. He assumed that the only way to assure that the lower production costs of hydroelectric power would be passed along to consumers was for the public sector to control and develop it. Smith's aide, Robert Moses, drafted a bill creating the first state power authority in the nation, but the utilities' influence in the legislature was much too strong and the bill was defeated.

Franklin Roosevelt picked up the cause after he succeeded Smith as Governor, but not until 1931, the last year of Roosevelt's administration, did the power authority bill become law. Like many of Roosevelt's accomplishments in the state, the passage of the bill was mainly a symbolic victory. The legislature refused to finance the authority. Herbert Lehman, Roosevelt's successor, also failed to make it operative. George Courtelyou and his allies not only thwarted three governors' efforts to establish a power authority; at the same time they paved the way for private hydroelectric projects and interconnecting transmission lines. The new power authority remained dormant until 1952, when Governor Thomas E. Dewey demonstrated an excellent sense of history, as well as determination, by appointing Robert Moses as its chairman.

During his frustrated efforts to get New York State into

the power business, Roosevelt waged a war of words with Consolidated Gas. The principal issue was still utility rates. Roosevelt's aide, Louis Howe, prepared a study showing that New York City customers paid more for their electricity than the residents of any other American city. The charge, which was and still is true, was rebutted by Courtelyou on the same ground that it is today. The higher rates, he explained, were based on the simple fact that it costs more to make and distribute electricity in New York. The higher costs in turn were caused by the city's underground transmission requirement, by the great number of apartment dwellers who consume less electricity than homeowners, and by the absence of large, twenty-four-hour industrial consumers.

Governor Roosevelt lost most of his battles with Consolidated Gas, but he began winning the war after he became President. The Tennessee Valley Authority, the Rural Electrification Administration, and the Public Utilities Holding Act are examples of New Deal reforms born of Roosevelt's New York experience. In his victory over Wendell Willkie in the 1940 election, Roosevelt also defeated one of the nation's foremost utility lawyers.

Roosevelt's successor, Governor Lehman, waged more limited skirmishes against the utilities, but the total of his small victories meant a saving of about $46 million in utility rates throughout the state during his first six years in office. Lehman, for example, introduced a requirement that the utilities pay interest every two years on customer deposits. Formerly Consolidated Gas and other utilities had held these cash advances, which protected the companies against unpaid bills, until a family moved or whenever gas or electric service was terminated. It became, in effect, a major source of interest-free loans to the utilities.

Of all the public officials who campaigned against the financial power and rates of Consolidated Gas, none conducted himself more colorfully than Mayor Fiorello La Guardia. On his very first day in office La Guardia lashed out at the company, imperiously demanding that electric bills be lowered. When that didn't work, he announced that the city would build "yardstick" plants to check on how much it actually cost to produce electricity. "The fight for a yardstick municipal plant is bound to be a bitter struggle," La Guardia predicted, "in which the utility interests use their great wealth and power to defend themselves against any threat to their profits." La Guardia prophesied correctly, for after he secured the City Council's approval of a referendum on municipal plants, gas company lawyers took the referendum to court, where they convinced the judge that La Guardia was tampering with the rights given to the company under the original gas franchises. La Guardia responded to his defeat by imposing a 1.5 percent gross receipts tax on Consolidated Gas, claiming that the company was charging the city "30 to 40 percent more" for street lighting than other cities paid. La Guardia won that round in 1936 when the rates were reduced.

In their confrontations with Consolidated Gas, the elected state officials from Smith to La Guardia attacked the tip of the bureaucratic iceberg, assuming that the financiers at the top were running things when in fact the engineer managers below were in control. Rates and centralized financial power were interpreted as the key issues because they were what consumers either saw or feared. The Depression sharpened this focus, as did the memory of the robber barons, whose quest for immortality had been successful enough to convince Americans that they were still around, greedy as ever.

While the profit motive surely did account for rate increases and the growth of Consolidated Gas, the means by which the company strengthened its monopoly position and expanded in size and influence were provided by the engineer managers. Their full emergence in the company occurred in 1935, when George Courtelyou retired. Courtelyou was the last chief executive who could accurately be described as a generalist. His successors were specialists, principally engineers, drawn from the company ranks. During his twenty-nine-year reign Courtelyou was a front man for the specialists, paving the political path for their gadgets and technical requirements and presiding over their ascendancy within the company. While he dealt they built. They created a large and modern electrical system, including nine power stations, two East River tunnels, several hundred miles of underground transmission cables, and the company headquarters, suitably called the "Tower of Light," at 4 Irving Place, across from Lüchow's Restaurant on 14th Street. With the exception of two generators installed after World War II, this is the basic service system that keeps New York City running today.

Courtelyou bridged two different periods of company history: its formation by the robber barons and its growth under the technical specialists. When the specialists took over from Courtelyou, they chucked the symbols of the past by renaming the company Consolidated Edison in honor of the engineer inventor. That was in 1936. Between 1936 and World War II Con Edison rose to its greatest strength and prominence. The new leaders rejoiced with the famous "City of Light" exhibit at the New York World's Fair in 1939. The exhibit portrayed the engineering and technical view of the man-made environment: a miniature and therefore manageable New York City brilliantly illuminated by thousands of tiny lights and efficiently run by thousands of machines. Americans approved. The "City of Light" was the biggest attraction at the fair. Then came World War II, and the lights were dimmed.

The postwar power problems of Con Edison are often explained by company critics as the result of greedy promotion. The company, it is said, pushed people into using more electricity than it eventually could provide. This narrow explanation ignores two more profound reasons that reveal a great deal not only about Con Edison but about American society. The first was World War II. The war economy directed virtually all production to airplanes, tanks, and other military hardware. Nothing was left for schools, railroads, houses, or power plants. Many of the nation's current urban problems may be traced to the hiatus in new construction and maintenance caused by World War II. The United States simply never caught up with the pent-up demands that exploded during the postwar years. In Con Edison's case an entire cycle of new plant construction was blacked out. Maintenance was deferred. In 1946 the newest plant in the system was thirty years old. The company was unprepared and too weak to handle the new surge in electrical consumption.

The second basic cause of Con Edison's problem was the pattern of postwar electrical consumption. During the 1930s the peak demands occurred during the night, and the seasonal high was in the winter. The principal users of electricity were families and the main function of electricity was lighting. The older employees at Con Edison's control center recall nostalgically that the biggest electrical demand usually occurred on Christmas Eve and on Christmas night, apparently because of toy trains and decorations.

During the postwar years demand leveled out between day and night, an obvious shift in heavy usage from the home to the office. Engineer managers in other companies were creating and using machines powered by electricity, and workers organized their functions to take advantage of computers, high-speed calculators, duplicators, and other new office equipment.

The machines released enormous quantities of heat in office buildings, as did the new banks of fluorescent lights ordered by architects who seldom questioned the requirements set by the Illuminating Engineering Society. The Society, influenced heavily by the lighting manufacturers, since 1949 has almost doubled its interior lighting standards, which make no allowance for daylight. Massive ventilating and air conditioning systems became essential not only to remove the heat created by lights and office equipment but because of the architects' insistence on creating controlled building environments and their use of exterior walls with windows that would not open.

Developers responded to the space needs of the machines and the prestige requirements of corporations by constructing a vast array of new office buildings in the postwar years. Old areas of the city, such as Third Avenue, became urban trenches lined with glass buildings. Some of the larger structures consumed as much electricity as a middle-sized American city.

By 1957 the office buildings completely overturned the traditional pattern of electrical consumption. The peak demands on Con Edison generators now occurred during the days, particularly in the summer, when the air conditioners were on. These daytime demands were three times greater than the old nighttime peaks for which the Con Edison system was designed. The company was in trouble.

Recent technical reports of the Federal Power Commission, the New York State Public Service Commission, and the City of New York describe in great detail the dawning of New York City's power problems, including the major role played by office towers. Upon reading these reports one is amazed that the blackouts and brownouts of the 1960s did not occur sooner. Among the conditions for earlier disaster were the sheer size and disorganization of Con Edison—20,000 employees housed in twenty-four affiliates, each with a separate board and staff, and an abundance of vice-presidents with little more to do than keep their chauffeurs and secretaries busy. It was hard to get anything accomplished at Con Edison. Another problem was the lack of adequate interconnections with other utilities to import emergency electricity in case of major power failures. Those ties that did exist presumed that Con Edison would sell some excess electricity to other utilities, not import it in large amounts.

Con Edison held up as long as it did because of the familiarity, even affection, of many plant employees for the old generators they minded. Another reason was the dramatic effort of the company during the 1950s to make the system survive.

The role of the plant employees is best introduced by a comment Thomas Edison made in 1910 about large electrical equipment. Edison pointed out that because many generators are custom made, it is really impossible to prepare a useful operating and maintenance manual for them. The reliability of a generator, he said, can be assured only by the men who mind it. An interesting bond develops between a man and a machine, especially if a worker spends a lifetime lubricating, cleaning, and maintaining it. In the process he learns its quirks, when to turn it off before it burns a bearing, and how to keep it going in emergencies. Some of the people who work at Con Edison power stations can trace their ancestors to the first gas works. Operating a generator in some cases is actually a family tradition. There is a lot of inbreeding at Con Edison. A 1960 report of the Con Edison personnel office showed that 90 percent of the employees had been referred to the company by existing employees, many of whom were relatives. Inbreeding has been cited in U.S. Civil Rights Commission reports as a cause of racial discrimination. While that may be so, other government reports indicate that inbreeding kept the Con Edison system working far longer than anyone had a right to expect.

The executive who kept Con Edison running in the race with crisis was Hudson ("Roy") Searing, who became chairman in 1953, when he and other engineers began to see clearly that the company's power picture was not bright. Searing was a typical midcentury Con Edison executive. He entered the company in 1909 and worked for a while as a draftsman; after getting an engineering degree, he rose to become a vice-president for engineering.

Searing launched a major construction program in the 1950s. Two new plants were built in Staten Island and Queens, and while they were under way Searing oversaw the planning of two of the boldest projects ever undertaken by a private utility: the nation's first private nuclear plant at Indian Point and the largest oil-fired plant in the nation, the 1,000-megawatt "Big

Allis" plant at Ravenswood, named for the Allis Chalmers Company, which built it. His strategy was to erect the biggest plants possible and to centralize their construction on large sites. There was no time to fiddle around with small plants on scattered sites.

In 1954 Searing had purchased a 380-acre park on the Hudson River in Westchester County from the bankrupt Day Line, where he planned to build not just one but several nuclear plants. To avoid delays, he decided, the federal government and other utilities would not be involved. Con Edison would finance, build, test, and run its own nuclear plants.

Searing entered the race against crisis too late. On June 26, 1957—before his bolder plans were realized—the dials portraying electrical consumption at Con Edison's control center hit an all-time high of 3,460 megawatts (a megawatt equals one million watts). It was not only the highest peak ever but the first time the peak load had occurred in the daylight hours, and the company's generators could not keep up with it. Calls went out around eight that morning to neighboring utilities. New Jersey Public Service and Long Island Lighting said they could help. Electricity came in through the wires that had been made for export. That afternoon Roy Searing died.

Tragedy and humiliation mark June 26, 1957. Con Edison lost a strong leader and was finally overtaken by the same forces of economic growth, bureaucracy, and technology that had built it and that would now converge to produce the battle of Storm King Mountain.

THE PLAN

In 1960 a group of about ten engineers at Con Edison was given the specialized and urgent assignment of determining how a hydroelectric pumped-storage plant could help stave off the impending power crisis in New York City. Their leader was Motton L. Waring, then Con Edison's vice-president for engineering.

Waring is a mild-mannered man in his fifties, regarded by his peers as a competent engineer and an agreeable man. His farm in Virginia, where he was raised, and his home in Ardsley-on-Hudson reveal that away from his office Waring has

THE PLAN

many interests and talents. He is an accomplished cabinet maker and gardener. Birds swarm through his garden to eat safely at feeders that Waring designed to be squirrel proof. At his office Waring devoted his energy to the Storm King project, the culmination of a career that began at Con Edison during the Depression, after he graduated from engineering school.

Waring's friendship with the late Hudson Searing increased his dedication to the assignment. Pumped-storage plants are ideal supplements to the large base generators that Searing had planned during the 1950s. These generators, which were installed to meet the company's peak demand periods during the daylight hours, went unused at night, when the demand dropped sharply. With a pumped-storage plant one or two of the larger generators could be kept running, and their power could be transmitted to a pumping station, which would draw water to a high elevation and store it in a reservoir. When additional power was needed the return water flow would be forced by gravity through turbines. The requirements for hydroelectric pumped storage include a dependable water source, a nearby high elevation to which the water can be pumped, and a natural basin or man-made reservoir in which the water can be stored. From the perspective of an engineer, the Hudson Highlands are custom made for pumped storage.

The development of such plants was hampered until the introduction in 1960 of a reversible turbine—that is, a machine that can both pump water and be energized by the return flow. Previously separate pumping and generating facilities were necessary, and some of the earlier plants proved to be uneconomical. According to Waring, the new turbine became available around the same time that he received a telephone call from the chief engineer of Central Hudson Gas and Electric in Newburgh, who suggested that Con Edison investigate the pumped-storage possibilities at Storm King. Central Hudson's engineers had been studying the area for several months but had found that the potential development costs and generating capacity of a plant on Storm King Mountain were too much for them to handle. Instead, the Central Hudson engineers had decided to confine their interests to Breakneck Ridge, across from Storm King, where they planned to build a modest pumped-storage plant sometime in the future. In the meantime, the smaller utility would support Con Edison's entry at Storm King, which lies in Central Hudson's service area, by agreeing to purchase some of the electricity and working with local officials to secure the necessary approvals.

Central Hudson was using the engineering firm of Uhl, Hall, and Rich. Waring signed up the consultants to continue their work for Con Edison. Borings, site surveys, studies of river flow, and preliminary land-cost appraisals were undertaken. Memoranda were prepared on the clearances required from public agencies. Site plans were drawn for the location of the reservoir, tunnel, powerhouse, and water intake. Tie-ins to the Con Edison system were designed, schematic drawings of the facilities were prepared, and rough estimates were compiled on construction costs.

This complicated bureaucratic process was also a creative one for Waring and his associates. From their instructions, telephone calls, memoranda, and meetings emerged the pieces of the Storm King project and their personal commitment to it. By 1962 they had given birth to an idea that, unknown to them, would greatly affect the Hudson Valley in the next ten years, even though the project never proceeded beyond the blueprint stage.

The site they had chosen for the storage reservoir was two miles west of the river in a basin created by the slopes of Mount Misery and White Horse Mountain. With the erection of five earthen dikes, the basin would be transformed into a 240-acre reservoir with a capacity of 8 billion gallons. A tunnel forty feet in diameter would be sunk to sea level 1,000 feet below and would then be cut eastward under Route 9W and Storm King Mountain for two miles to the riverside powerhouse. Geology studies indicated that the granite of Storm King could support such an extensive cavity, and that seepage from both the tunnel and the reservoir would be minimal. This was a major consideration, since the brackish river water could pollute the local water table.

Finding a location for the riverside powerhouse and intake tunnel was a bit of a problem. One possibility was a site several hundred feet to the south of the base of Storm King Mountain on land owned by the Palisades Interstate Park Commission. Private hydroelectric power plants constructed on navigable waterways require a license from the Federal Power Commission, and the license, once granted, carries with it the power of eminent domain over state and city park lands. The problem with the park site was not legal, but political. Laurance Rockefeller, the brother of New York's Governor, was chairman of the New York State Parks Council and a member of the Palisades Interstate Park Commission. Mr. Rockefeller's reaction to having a portion of his park carved out for a powerhouse was uncertain.

A second possible site was the Cornwall waterfront on the northern side of the mountain. It was privately owned and contained the remnants of Cornwall's past as a major river resort town including the rotted piers of the dock where the *Mary Powell,* the swiftest and most famous of the Hudson's steamers, once landed. Then there were the Eureka Hotel, the stone basement of Lillian Russell's summer cottage, portions of the old West Shore line railroad station, and a store where Willie Hoppe, a local boy, first learned to play pool. During the twentieth century Cornwall residents abandoned the waterfront, leaving behind the old buildings like the molt from an earlier period of development. There was no reason to believe that the owners of waterfront land would object to selling their property and then seeing it razed to make way for the powerhouse and intake tunnel.

Curiously enough, Waring was concerned less with Cornwall's reaction to this site than with what New York City officials might say, for, it turned out, 40 percent of New York's water supply passes beneath Cornwall. In fact, the Moodna Tunnel section of the Catskill Aqueduct, which conveys water from the Ashokan Reservoir, was located directly under the potential Con Edison site. The tunnel, which runs 220 feet beneath the base of Storm King Mountain and then descends to 1,100 feet under the Hudson River en route to the Kensico Reservoir in Westchester County, was only 173 feet away from the company's proposed powerhouse. New York City normally forbids any drilling or excavation within 200 feet of the tunnel because it is a critical link in its water supply system and is maintained under constant hydrostatic pressure.

At the time Waring felt that if the Cornwall site were chosen he could get the necessary permission from the city's Bureau of Water Supply. What he did not count on was the intervention of Carmine De Sapio, the Democratic political leader in

New York, who apparently took a keen interest in aqueduct matters. In 1970 De Sapio was convicted of demanding personal payments from Con Edison contractors for permission to build on aqueduct rights of way. Waring and his associates strenuously disclaim any direct dealings with De Sapio. They say only that after James Marcus became Water Commissioner in the Lindsay administration it often took two years to get replies to their letters about the Cornwall project.

According to Waring, the trustees of Con Edison were fully committed to the general outline of the Storm King project by early 1962 after he briefed them on the engineering studies. The reports showed that 2,000 megawatts of excess, off-peak capacity could be switched from the company's base generators to a pumping station at Storm King, and that during a seventeen-hour period this energy would fill the 8-billion-gallon reservoir. Once released and passed through the powerhouse, the stored water could generate 2,000 megawatts of electricity for eleven hours, which is roughly the amount of power that New York City once demanded during the highest period of electrical consumption before World War II.

The project, it should be stressed, did not offer a new source of electricity, but merely the storage of unused generating capacity from Con Edison's base generators. For every three units of electricity transferred to Storm King two units would be returned. Among the advantages of the project was that within three minutes it could provide energy for periods up to eleven hours in emergencies, for sale to other utilities, or as a supplement to the company's New York City generators. Waring told the trustees that the project would take five years and about $162 million to build. They authorized him to proceed.

Large development plans are normally kept under wraps

until their creators feel they have answered some of the major questions that may crop up. Corporate planners are especially mindful of the effect of a premature announcement on land costs. The Rouse Company, developers of the new town of Columbia, Maryland, for instance, never revealed its intentions until most of the 165 farms on the Columbia site were acquired separately. The Rouse staff feels that if the idea had been publicized in advance, the budgeted acquisition price of $1,500 per acre would have doubled, and Columbia would have never been built.

By the spring of 1962 Con Edison and its smaller partner, Central Hudson Gas and Electric, were sitting on some rather dramatic plans. Without informing the public, they proposed to transform Storm King Mountain and Breakneck Ridge, the historic gateway to the Hudson Highlands, into twin hydroelectric projects. The secrecy with which the two utilities developed their plans would eventually become a major issue in the debate over Storm King Mountain. From the companies' point of view, however, it could be argued that their secret was not maintained long enough. For as we shall see, by the summer of 1962 news of the project began leaking before Waring had answered the major questions about the plant. As a result, he began reacting to rather than shaping events.

The first elected politician to be apprised of the Con Edison plan was Michael ("Doc") Donohue, the mayor of the village of Cornwall-on-Hudson. Cornwall-on-Hudson is a jurisdiction within the larger town of Cornwall. While both the village and the town would be affected by Con Edison's plan, the proposed sites for the powerhouse and storage reservoir were in the village. Under the plan the projected storage reservoir

THE PLAN

would submerge the main reservoir of the village which also supplies water to the town. Mayor Donohue would have to go along with the sacrifice.

Donohue is typical of the mayors who serve the towns and villages along the river. He has held office for twenty years, often running unopposed for reelection. He serves only part time. Donohue is a veterinarian, and he fulfills his official duties by showing up an hour each morning at the village hall and attending some evening meetings. He is also available to discuss village business on the veranda of his home beneath Storm King Mountain before the evening rush of clients with ailing animals.

With the exception of a metal fastener plant, neither the village nor town of Cornwall has a large taxpaying industry. Many of its citizens are retired staff members of the West Point Military Academy and therefore have veterans' tax exemptions. Education is the town's principal industry. It is the home of three college preparatory schools: the New York Military Academy, the Braden School, and the Storm King School. Cornwall's frail economy is tied to that of Newburgh, one of New York State's most troubled small cities.

Like most river mayors, Donohue has no time or interest in the subtleties of municipal planning. His exclusive priority is keeping down local taxes, and judging by his long term in office the local electorate feels the same way. Mayor Donohue seems prepared to accept any change in Cornwall that will expand his tax base.

Donohue recalls that it was sometime in the late summer of 1962 that he was "summoned" to the Newburgh headquarters of Central Hudson Gas and Electric, where Waring, flanked by Central Hudson executives and some of his staff, including a public relations man, broke the news about the Storm King project. Donohue remembers being bothered by the format of the announcement. He was also surprised that Con Edison had managed to proceed so far with its planning without someone in Cornwall finding out.

The mayor says that his first concern was how the townsfolk would react to going to bed at night with all that water being held up in the mountains by some dirt dikes. But the most troublesome aspect of the project was the loss of the village reservoir, which had been given to Cornwall by one of the wealthy families who lived on Storm King. The reservoir was a dependable source of clear and delicious spring water, not the kind of resource a mayor discards lightly. But then there were the potential tax revenues of the plant to consider, estimated at about a million dollars a year. That was more than half of Cornwall's town and village budget and would represent a net gain since the plant required no local services. Waring also pointed out that Con Edison would finance a replacement for the reservoir. Donohue replied that he would like some time to consider the project.

Donohue, in fact, could barely contain his euphoria over having a major tax-producing industry dropped into his lap. He says that after leaving the meeting with Waring, his only real concern was whether the company could be trusted. He had read about Con Edison's arsenal of nuclear plants at Indian Point, which was reported to have brought riches to the village of Cornwall, located on the east bank of the Hudson River just south of Peekskill in Westchester County. He telephoned the mayor of Buchanan, William Burke, to arrange a private meeting so they could compare notes on Con Edison.

THE PLAN

Mayor Burke recalls that Donohue arrived at the Buchanan village hall in a squad car chauffeured by Cornwall's police chief. The time was the first or second week in September, 1962. The two mayors, meeting for the first time, struck it off well, and Burke gladly outlined Con Edison's contributions to the life of Buchanan.

Con Edison came to Buchanan in 1954, when the Hudson River Day Line was about to sell Indian Point Park, a recreation stop for river cruises. The most interested buyer was a housing developer who proposed turning the entire 340 acres into residential use. Burke, who had recently been elected mayor and was also business manager in the local school district, quickly realized that the developer's plans would place a heavy burden on the schools, drain the village budget, and possibly introduce some unwanted new neighbors.

When Hudson Searing of Con Edison expressed an interest in the park in 1954, Burke switched the zoning of the area to industrial, then negotiated five successive nuclear plants on Indian Point and adjacent land. Three of the plants were agreed to before the first two were even finished. By 1970 Con Edison accounted for $34,380,000 of the village's total assessed valuation of $38,358,839.

With Con Edison's tax money, which is actually far less than the company would have to pay for comparable plants in New York City or in localities more affluent than Buchanan, Mayor Burke maintained the tax rate while investing in a vast array of municipal improvements, including three off-street parking lots, two tennis courts, new fire plugs, a sewage treatment plant, the repaving of all village streets, and the installation of new mercury arc street lights.

What Mayor Burke could not tell Mayor Donohue in

1962 were some of the problems that would arise in Buchanan by 1971, including the maze of transmission lines that run over Buchanan's main street, the expenditure of $400,000 for a new road to handle the traffic to and from the plant, and Con Edison's ownership of half the village, including all of its waterfront. Yet judging by Burke's numerous reelections most people in Buchanan do not mind these problems, nor are they apparently concerned by the presence of five nuclear plants, as long as the taxes stay down. Meanwhile, Mayor Burke has expanded his ambassadorial duties and now makes speeches around the nation on how Buchanan has benefited from the nuclear age.

Mayor Donohue returned to Cornwall like a conquering hero. His jubilation over the project plus Burke's reassurances about Con Edison placed the mayor firmly on the company's side. But now, of course, Donohue was a substantial security risk. So on September 27, 1962, the company's public relations staff released the story of the project to the press. The news received front-page treatment in *The New York Times*. From this point on Waring proceeded on the basis of an announced project, although the details of what would happen next were not very clear to the public, nor were they, it seems, to Waring.

With the exception of labor and political leaders in Orange County who expressed pleasure over the possible economic benefits of the plant for Newburgh and Cornwall, there was no widespread reaction to the news. In Cornwall, of course, local leaders were vying with Mayor Donohue in claiming credit for bringing Con Edison to town, and there was even some enthusiastic talk about eliminating all local taxes on residential property. But elsewhere there was silence, which at the time seemed not at all strange, to Waring at least. Impressed only by the logic and benefits of the plant, Waring foresaw no problems in public acceptance.

Some unexpected flak arose shortly after the announcement when Waring met with the Palisades Interstate Park Commission. Laurance Rockefeller and the other commissioners were annoyed at having to read about the project in the newspapers, especially since Con Edison was thinking about using park land for the powerhouse. Waring placated the commissioners by offering to move the powerhouse to the Cornwall side of the mountain, a step that he assumed would meet with the approval of Mayor Donohue since the powerhouse would provide even more tax benefits to Cornwall.

The commissioners also expressed their displeasure over the location of the plant's transmission lines, a feature of the project that consumed much of Waring's time for the remainder of 1962. As outlined in the preliminary designs, the transmission lines would be suspended across the Storm King gorge on two immense towers erected on concrete abutments. After crossing the river, the lines would be strung to a substation about three quarters of a mile inland, then east across Putnam County for about ten miles to a major north-south transmission link connecting the Niagara Mohawk Power Company's system in upstate New York with Con Edison's facilities in New York City.

In addition to the Palisades Park commissioners, two other prominent local leaders expressed concern over the power lines. One was the commandant of the West Point Military Academy, William Westmoreland, who was worried that the transmission apparatus would interfere with landing approaches to the now defunct Stewart Air Force Base in Newburgh. General Westmoreland also pointed out that the lines across the Storm

King gorge interfered with the normal helicopter route from the air base to the academy.

An aesthetic objection to the towers and lines across the gorge was brought to Waring's attention by William Osborn, president of the Hudson River Conservation Society and the brother of one of the Palisades Park commissioners, Frederick Osborn. William had personal reasons for objecting. At the end of the living room of his country home in Garrison is an enormous window that looks out on the gorge in the distance. But his position on the power line question was based on more than merely glancing out the window.

Like many of the wealthy families who have retreats in the Hudson Highlands, the Osborns regarded the Con Edison project as a test of their social responsibility. With the exception of the taxpayers of Cornwall, virtually no one in the highlands really welcomed the plant. The question, as it was debated by the Osborns and others, was whether they should make the sacrifice of allowing the plant in the interest of permitting the hordes in New York City to enjoy the benefits of lower-cost electricity. The Osborns decided that it was a proper sacrifice, provided that the lines across the gorge were eliminated. In view of the fact that the Osborns held key official posts in two important local institutions, their decision was significant.

The Hudson River Conservation Society, of which William was president, is a genteel organization formed during the Depression by wealthy river families for the purpose of continuing under private auspices the battle they had begun in 1900, with formation of the Palisades Park Commission, to protect scenic river lands from commercial encroachment. The specific enemies of the society were the quarry men, who were leveling the highlands at a steady rate. By the 1960s the society had fallen into bad times. Its total assets were a mere $16,000, and its interests had become a matter more of which battle had been fought where than of what the developers were doing.

Osborn was determined to revive the society as a constructive organization that would work with Con Edison to minimize the scenic disruption of its Storm King plant. The idea was to achieve the "multiple use" of natural resources, a major theme in Laurance Rockefeller's various conservation activities. Rockefeller therefore joined the two Osborns in their efforts to persuade Waring to modify the plant design by at least eliminating the clothesline effect across the Storm King gorge. The implication was that in return Waring would receive the support of the Conservation Society and Laurance Rockefeller. The following year, 1965, Rockefeller and the Osborns became the leading local boosters of Con Edison's plans, and the Hudson River Conservation Society voted not to oppose the project.

For Waring, working with the president of the Conservation Society and the Palisades Park commissioners was an exercise in democratic planning. He was bending to local interests by making some significant and costly changes in his project. In January 1963 Con Edison announced that it would eliminate the towers and overhead lines across the gorge. The company promised to use submarine cable, at a total added cost of $6 million.

Following the power line concession, which Waring assumed would pave the way for complete local acceptance of the project, the Con Edison vice-president plunged into specific negotiations with three diverse interests: Harvard University, New York City's Bureau of Water Supply, and Cornwall's Mayor Donohue.

Harvard entered the picture because the Stillman family

had given the university the Black Rock Forest, a portion of which would be submerged by the planned reservoir to the rear of Storm King Mountain. Harvard offered no official opposition, although its administrators were annoyed at the manner in which Con Edison broke the news. Someone at Con Edison— Waring denies it was he—called Harvard officials and suggested that they meet at a Howard Johnson's located between Boston and New York to discuss the Black Rock Forest—hardly the most diplomatic way of broaching the subject.

New York City's interest in the project concerned the aqueduct right of way beneath the Cornwall site. Discussions with city officials in 1963 resulted in no indications of the De Sapio-Marcus intrigues that were to come later in the decade. The Bureau of Water Supply simply notified Con Edison that a construction permit would be required.

Discussions with Cornwall led to some elaborate and bizarre arrangements concerning the village reservoir. As Waring expected, Mayor Donohue was pleased to learn that the village would also get the powerhouse, particularly since Con Edison agreed to pay full assessment taxes on the waterfront property until it was ready to build.

As part of the deal, Waring also offered to build a waterfront park for Cornwall on rockfill removed from the mountain for the tunnel. The rockfill would be deposited in the river, extending the existing Cornwall waterfront by 300 feet into the Hudson for a distance of one mile. The company would cover the deposits with earth, plant some trees, and erect a visitors center for the plant. The park also provided a convenient means for Con Edison to get rid of its excavation wastes.

On the key issue of the reservoir, Waring offered to finance a replacement, including a village well, a new filtration plant, a tap on the Catskill Aqueduct, and necessary water mains, at an estimated cost of $3 million. It should be explained that twenty-three other towns along the right of way already had taps on the aqueduct. One problem that arose during these negotiations was how to sidestep a state law requiring villages to hold a referendum before disposing of their water supplies. The local assemblyman was asked to introduce special legislation in Albany releasing Cornwall from the requirement. The bill was routinely passed during the 1963 session of the legislature.

Negotiating the fine details of the reservoir replacement required numerous and prolonged discussions, more than could be expected of a part-time mayor. Waring therefore offered to reimburse the village for the expenses of Cornwall's attorney in the negotiations, Raymond Bradford. Waring now stresses that this offer was made with the full knowledge and authority of Con Edison's trustees. The impropriety of the arrangement, which after all meant that Bradford was being paid by the same company he was negotiating with on behalf of the village, was compounded when Bradford submitted some of his bills directly to Con Edison. Adding to the problem was the fact that in 1964 Bradford began rounding up witnesses and preparing testimony in support of Con Edison's project before the Federal Power Commission. The source and method of Bradford's payments, which amounted to $138,000, were publicized in 1968 by a reporter from the nearby *Middletown Record.*

By March 1963 Con Edison was proceeding at full speed. The license application was submitted to the FPC, and various company officials began briefing key public leaders to win their blessing for the project. High on the list was Governor Nelson

Rockefeller. One path leading to the grandson of John D. Rockefeller was lined with labor leaders, principally Peter Brennan, head of the state's building tradesmen, and Harry Van Arsdale, leader of New York City's taxi cab drivers and the titular head of city union organizations. Van Arsdale's and Brennan's support were virtually automatic. Orange County union leaders were solidly behind the project; in addition, labor normally boosts Con Edison projects, which, from excavations to plant additions, accounted for about 15 percent of the construction employment in the New York City area in the early 1960s. Given labor's endorsement, plus his brother's participation in the siting and transmission line negotiations, Governor Rockefeller also became an automatic supporter of the project.

On March 12, 1963, the FPC issued a public notice of the license application, giving interested persons for or against the plant until April 29, 1963, to file their intentions. No one indicated any objections. The silence may be attributed to the fact that the notice was published only in the Federal Register and in an obscure weekly newspaper in Goshen, New York, many miles from the project site. But a more fundamental explanation is that there was at the time no precedent for large-scale opposition to a project of this kind either in the history of the river or in contemporary American affairs. Elsewhere, American cities and landscapes were being vastly altered not just by urban renewal or highway programs but by the force of post-World War II urbanization, of which the Storm King project was only one example. Waring and his associates were completely justified in assuming at the time that their project was merely business as usual, and that there would be at most just isolated resistance.

But a fuse was lit at the Con Edison stockholders meeting

in May 1963 when the company distributed its annual report. The report contained the first detailed sketch of the Storm King plant. The author of the sketch demonstrated the often unappreciated power of the artist, for by showing what the company would do to Storm King Mountain he did more than anyone else to create the beginnings of the opposition. His picture showed a portion of Storm King missing, like a slice removed from a tub of cheese. In its place was Waring's power plant, a glistening, sharp-edged steel-and-concrete structure contrasted against what remained of the natural beauty of the mountain. The unknown artist had visualized the contradictions and conflicts of river history.

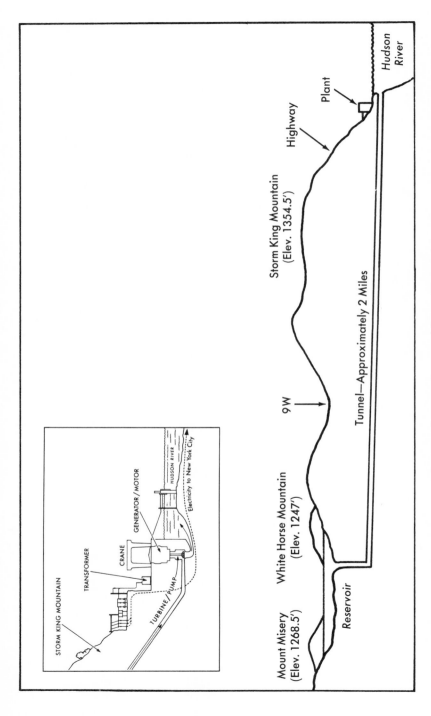

Cutaway diagram of proposed Storm King project.

CONFLICT

The publication of the plant sketch in May 1963 had its first impact in the villages across the river from Storm King, particularly in Cold Spring and Garrison, where there was already considerable anxiety about the transmission lines. Some property owners were more peeved than relieved by the compromise of submerging the lines across the gorge. Why, they wondered, couldn't the lines across their property also be buried? With the publication of the sketch, east bank residents got an idea of what they would have to look at. They were doubly annoyed.

Although the complaints from the east bank villages failed

at first to produce any organized opposition, they did produce some angry spokesmen. One was a Garrison antiques dealer, Benjamin Frazier, who is also a local history buff and the director of the restoration of Boscobel, the Robert Adams-designed house that is now a highlight in any historical tour of the highlands. Another major spokesman was Alexander Saunders, who owns a manufacturing business in nearby Nelsonville and, like Frazier, is a permanent and well-known resident of the area.

Con Edison's proposal both angered and frustrated the two men. There seemed to be nothing they could do to stop the project, except to find others in the Hudson Valley who might share their opposition. Their search led to the formation of a small, informal, and ineffectual band of opponents during the months following the announcement of the project.

The organizers were Walter Boardman, then director of the Nature Conservancy, and Leo Rothschild, a New York City attorney who also served as president of the New York–New Jersey Trail Conference. The announcement of the plant was a rude shock for Boardman and Rothschild, who had been surveying the highlands to determine whether scenic sites in the area were threatened by commercial or industrial development. The Nature Conservancy, using foundation and private contributions, buys endangered scenic lands. With Con Edison's announcement, the two men realized there was not much time for study. The Trail Conference was especially concerned by the possible loss of Storm King Mountain since some of the hiking paths it maintains in the area faced the same fate as Cornwall's reservoir and Harvard's forest.

Boardman and Rothschild contacted their friends in various hiking, garden, and conservation groups, but the response

CONFLICT

was sluggish. After Con Edison's annual report came out, interest picked up. Novelist Carl Carmer, who lives in Irvington, joined the meetings, as did Frazier and Saunders from Garrison. There were even some feelers from the squires on Storm King Mountain, who despite their disapproval of Con Edison's plans remained strangely silent following the September 1962 announcement.

The quiet initial reaction of the "mountain people," as Mayor Donohue describes the families who have weekend homes on the mountain, is explained partly by the euphoria in town, where rumors were spreading about tax abatement. Calvin Stillman, a descendant of the former owner of Storm King, says that it took a good deal of courage even to question the plant in Cornwall.

One of the few early and outspoken critics was Mrs. Stephan ("Smokey") Duggan, whose mother had given Cornwall the reservoir that Donohue planned to sell to Con Edison. She was furious. Mr. Duggan recalls that he spent a good deal of time trying to calm his wife, explaining that corporate plans often go astray and that if Con Edison did go ahead the family had some legal remedies, including a state law forbidding the sale of its drinking supplies without a referendum.

Duggan, a Wall Street lawyer, spoke with considerable experience. He had represented the Gulf Oil Company in its controversial plan to construct an oil refinery in Narragansett Harbor. Duggan knew how corporation plans could get fouled up and was clearly not a conservation zealot. His transformation began when he read Con Edison's annual report, which suggested to him that the plant was moving ahead. Later, in the spring of 1964, he was shaken when a neighbor called asking

Duggan to represent him in litigation with Con Edison over the acquisition of well rights on his meadow. This was part of the reservoir deal. In the course of representing his neighbor, as well as his wife's interest in the village reservoir, Duggan learned that Cornwall had been exempted from the referendum requirement. From that point on Duggan became a leading opponent of Storm King and later was a founder of the Natural Resources Defense Council.

During 1963 the Cornwall opponents began speaking out against construction of the plant on their home ground, hoping to convince the Donohue administration and the townsfolk that the plant would ruin Cornwall and that the claims for the plant's tax and job benefits were exaggerated. They also argued that the village reservoir was too precious to be sacrificed for the project.

Mayor Donohue resented these arguments and their implied criticism of his negotiating abilities. He questioned the motives of the uplanders, who in addition to the Duggans consisted of about twenty families headed by New York City corporate executives, lawyers, and a retired Army general. Donohue charged that the "weekend crowd" cared more about the view from their windows than about the local school, police, and fire services, which would benefit from the plant taxes. Discussions soon broke down, and hard feelings developed between the plant opponents and the more numerous supporters. By the spring of 1964 the local opponents had given up their efforts at friendly persuasion in Cornwall and had cast their lot with the broader opposition being slowly organized by Rothschild and Boardman, for whom the technique of friendly persuasion had not worked either.

Following the publication of Con Edison's annual report, Carmer and Rothschild went to Con Edison and attempted to dissuade Waring from building his plant. Saunders wrote letters to Laurance Rockefeller, Secretary of the Interior Stewart Udall, and other public officials and was told that the project was beyond their power to stop. Another group met with Governor Rockefeller, who suggested that the adversaries buy the mountain.

In November 1963 the small band of opponents met at the home of Carl Carmer to review the disappointing results of their efforts. They had discovered that there was no "right person" to talk to about blocking the plant and now began examining the various bureaucratic checkpoints that Con Edison's plan would have to pass. At the time the only real public control over the siting and design of power plants was provided by building and zoning codes, the province of local officials. The role of most states was simply to comment on nuclear or hydroelectric projects whose licenses were under consideration by the Atomic Energy Commission or the FPC. The Army Corps of Engineers reviewed plans for plants built on navigable rivers, but the only purpose was to assure that there was no boating hazard.

The only bureaucratic pressure point for stopping the Storm King project was the FPC, whose record of refusing hydroelectric licenses for scenic or conservation purposes was slim.

The November meeting produced agreement that individual attempts were not going to work, and that to stop the plant a valleywide organization had to be set up to rally opposition and to wage a legal campaign against Con Edison's license application. The name chosen for the new organization was the

Scenic Hudson Preservation Conference. The odds against Scenic Hudson are suggested by the fact that there were only twelve people present at its founding during the November 1963 meeting.

The most pressing problem for Scenic Hudson's organizers was finding a lawyer to represent them at the FPC hearings on the license. The hearings were scheduled to begin in February, and under the commission's rules it was already too late to intervene.

The search for a lawyer was undertaken by Walter Boardman of the Nature Conservancy. He spent a month looking for a man who was familiar with the specialized administrative law of the FPC and who might conceivably take Scenic Hudson as a client. Finally, a friend in the Department of the Interior gave Boardman the name and phone number of Dale C. Doty, a Washington lawyer.

Doty, a Californian, had once worked for the Department of the Interior and the FPC. Between 1951 and 1953 he served as an FPC commissioner, and a signed photograph of Harry Truman, the President who appointed him, is among the few mementos and pictures hanging on the stark walls of his one-man law office on 13th Street in downtown Washington.

Doty's practice consists primarily of representing power companies before the FPC. He also helps the concessionaires in the national parks to deal with the Department of the Interior. Doty bends his practice to accommodate one or two "fights of principle," and the kind of fights that interest him are suggested by his record as an FPC commissioner.

Some of the older FPC employees still talk of how, in 1953, Doty singlehandedly maneuvered the FPC's refusal of a license application from the Namekagon Power Company, which wanted to construct a hydroelectric dam across the Namekagon, a small Wisconsin river. The proposed 380-foot dam, Doty felt, would have ruined the river for campers and fishermen. Doty, who has a quiet voice and a reputation for stubbornness, says that he bored his fellow commissioners into turning down the Namekagon Company's license application, the first time in FPC history that a refusal was issued on the basis of recreational reasons. The Namekagon Company appealed the decision, but it was sustained by a federal appeals court in 1954.

Doty knew about the Storm King case and was intrigued with some of the policy issues it raised. One of these was the FPC's preoccupation with economic and technical considerations. The agency had not paid heed to its Namekagon decision to establish firm scenic and recreational priorities. Another issue that Doty perceived at Storm King was the FPC's comprehensive plan requirement. Under its congressional mandate, the commission is required to assure that a projected private hydroelectric plant conforms to an overall plan for improving or developing a waterway. Doty surmised that if the Storm King application was like others that had appeared before the commission, no real relationship had been established between Con Edison's project and other developments along the river; rather it was simply a one-shot effort designed and then reviewed by civil and electrical engineers. Finally, Doty wanted to see more citizen pressure placed on the commission.

These interests were strong enough to persuade Doty to take on Scenic Hudson's case even though he had never seen the mountain, knew very little about his clients, and was entering the controversy at the last minute. Doty was first approached by Walter Boardman of the Nature Conservancy in January 1964, just three weeks before the FPC hearings were set to begin.

About all Doty had time for was the preparation and filing of the necessary papers for Scenic Hudson to intervene in the hearings.

Randall LeBoeuf, one of the nation's leading private utility lawyers and a partner in LeBoeuf, Lamb, and Leiby, the New York firm representing Con Edison at the FPC hearings, challenged Scenic Hudson's petition to intervene. LeBoeuf argued persuasively that ten months had passed since the deadline for filing intentions to appear at the hearing. He charged, in effect, that Scenic Hudson's petition was merely a last-minute effort by soreheads.

The FPC was in a quandary. The intervention of citizen groups was uncommon, and this one, as LeBoeuf claimed, seemed to offer nothing more than emergency opposition. On the other hand, the commission was receiving a lot of correspondence on the Storm King project and *The New York Times* had indicated interest in the hearings. Perhaps, some of the commissioners felt, it would be politic to allow some opponents to enter their comments into the hearing record. Furthermore, Doty was a respected counsel. Scenic Hudson was thus allowed to intervene in the hearings, though the atmosphere was barely cordial.

The scene during the first round of hearings suggested the tensions as well as the hurdles facing the opponents. The main section of the hearing room was filled with two busloads of Orange County building tradesmen. Their passage to Washington had been arranged by the Cornwall village attorney, Raymond Bradford, who was seated in front of them in the hearing room alongside Mayor Donohue. Close by were Waring and other Con Edison executives.

Three counsel tables were arranged at the front of the

room before the hearing examiner. One table was occupied by several young attorneys from LeBoeuf, Lamb, and Leiby who wrote furiously on yellow legal pads while their leader, LeBoeuf, moved around them, nodded approvals, and gave assignments. This body of talent would eventually cost Con Edison close to $8 million. At the second table were numerous staff representatives from the FPC. At the third table, sitting alone, was Doty, with a few Scenic Hudson members seated in the pews behind him.

The case for an FPC license is presented through scripts prepared by the applicant's counsel from information supplied by the experts who are called on to testify. Counsel and witness sometimes read their parts while the examiner and the opposing counsel follow what is being said from the scripts, thus making the prepared testimony some of the most intensively read literature in the English language. The purpose of this procedure is to establish an instant record that can be studied in advance for cross-examination by the opposing counsel or for questioning by the examiner. It is this aspect of the hearing that provides the only spontaneity and, occasionally, excitement.

LeBoeuf presented numerous witnesses who discussed the purpose of the plant, how it would work, the geology of the mountain, the transmission lines, plant costs, advantages, and need. The witnesses included executives of Consolidated Edison, employees of Uhl, Hall, and Rich, engineering consultants, and representatives of Cornwall and the neighboring area. It was a relentless presentation filled with the nuggets of information a hearing examiner is trained to listen for so that he can determine whether the application conforms to the requirements of the Federal Power Act. After several days of testimony, LeBoeuf

told the examiner that Con Edison had made a prima facie case
for the power plant. Now it was Doty's turn.

Up to this point Doty's performance had been lackluster.
Aside from making some procedural points such as suggesting
that the hearings be moved to New York City and questioning
the admission of certain letters in support of the plant, Doty
has remained silent during LeBoeuf's presentation, forgoing
the opportunity to cross-examine. He really had nothing to ask
the engineers, economists, and geologists, for, as he explained
later, he knew nothing of the details of Con Edison's plans. He
told the examiner that he would like a month or so to respond
to Con Edison's case with witnesses who would outline the scenic and historical significance of the Hudson Highlands and
present comments on the technical evidence offered on behalf of
the license application.

LeBoeuf parried the request for more time. "I can't see this
historical business at all," he said. "Why waste time having people tell us this is an historical area?" LeBoeuf had a point. The
FPC had never before paid much attention to history. On Doty's
request to present opposing technical testimony, LeBoeuf was
even more emphatic: "These matters exceed the grounds of Scenic Hudson's entry." In the hurried effort to make Scenic Hudson an intervenor, Doty had said nothing about the organization's technical interests. Doty persisted nonetheless, and the
examiner seemed reluctant to turn him down. A second round
of hearings was scheduled for May 1964.

During March and April of 1964 Doty, with the help of
some Scenic Hudson members, put together a case against the
use of Storm King Mountain for hydroelectric power. His arguments became the basis of Scenic Hudson's legal opposition for

the next seven years. They were a mixture of technical, economic, aesthetic, and spiritual considerations. It was a clever combination, but it demonstrated above all how difficult it is for a group of outsiders to challenge a large technological bureaucracy, particularly when a specialized administrative agency such as the FPC is sitting in judgment.

One of Doty's principal witnesses in the May hearings was a retired FPC engineer named Ellery Fosdick, whom Doty relied on to prove that there might be technical alternatives to a pumped-storage plant on Storm King Mountain. That Doty should use a retired engineer indicates the difficulty that citizen organizations often have in locating engineering firms to provide expert testimony. The costs are high, and many firms are reluctant to speak against a developer whom they would prefer to have as a client. Besides, most engineering firms would rather build than stop projects.

Fosdick suggested that portable gas turbines might be an alternative to pumped storage as a means of providing emergency peaking power. Although Fosdick's suggestion is bolstered by the fact that Con Edison has installed 2,000 megawatts of gas turbine power since 1965, largely to provide the peaking power that it hoped to get from Storm King, the former FPC man was demolished by LeBoeuf during cross-examination.

Another expert at the hearing was James Geraghty, a hydrologist, who explained that there might be some seepage of brackish Hudson River water from the reservoir and tunnel into the water table. LeBoeuf destroyed his testimony too by extracting the concession that seepage was a remote possibility and even the possibility was just one man's opinion.

As counterpoint to the technical testimony, Doty placed

some Scenic Hudson organizers on the stand to discuss why the mountain was important. Carl Carmer gave a brief historical sketch of the entire Hudson River and concluded by asking whether the river's national importance

> shall be sacrificed to these enterprises which would change the shoreline, lower high peaks, destroy groves of trees. If these threats are carried out, something of the quality in the American character will be replaced by an emptiness that can never be filled. . . . The Hudson answers a spiritual need, more necessary to the nation's health than all the commercial products it can provide, than all the money it can earn.

Frazier, the Garrison antiques dealer, discussed in greater detail the history of the Hudson Highlands. It was unfortunate for his purposes that Storm King does not satisfy normal American requirements for historical preservation. No great battle was fought there, and the more distinguished bones of the valley are buried elsewhere. But Frazier fitted Storm King into the broader highlands context, giving a verbal tour of the area, as he so often did from a boat during fund-raising drives for Scenic Hudson. He started the examiner at Bear Mountain on a northerly route, describing first the great chain that the revolutionaries had placed across the river in an unsuccessful attempt to stop the British frigates. Frazier went on to the Beverly Robinson House, which Benedict Arnold used as headquarters, and the Mandeville House, where George Washington stayed on various occasions. The next stop was Constitution Island, across from West Point, which was the first Hudson River site fortified by the Americans and which still contained many of the old redoubts and batteries. It was here that a second and successful chain was laid across the river, and where Washington bade farewell to his personal staff. On an actual boat tour Frazier can become so inspired by the island that his narrative falls behind. Even in the hearing room he rushed through his description of the next landmark, Cold Spring, where the nation's principal Civil War ironworks, the West Point Foundry, was located. Then came Boscobel, the early American house that Frazier had almost personally reassembled on a Cold Spring site. He concluded his narrative with a description of the east bank and the guardian of that rich, nostalgic area, Storm King Mountain.

LeBoeuf slashed through Frazier's testimony with enthusiasm. "You claim," he said, "that Washington's thoughts were continually on the highlands during the war. How do you know that?" Frazier replied that the Hudson Highlands were strategically important and therefore must have been on the general's mind. LeBoeuf proceeded with a more interesting line of attack, pointing out that highlands residents might well have regarded the West Point Foundry and the military academy as severe intrusions into the natural landscape, yet with time they became important historical landmarks. LeBoeuf then raised the question of whether the Storm King plant might not achieve the same status. At a future hearing the same question was asked of Charles Callison of the Audubon Society, who unlike Frazier was prepared with a reply. "Yes," he conceded sarcastically, "it would mark the beginning of a new era of history in the highlands."

LeBoeuf's rebuttal to Scenic Hudson's case dwelled mainly on technical issues, particularly on the claim that gas turbines were a suitable alternative to the Storm King project.

Con Edison executives and consultants returned to the stand to argue that turbines were more costly and less reliable than hydroelectric power. They testified that a pumped-storage plant could respond more efficiently than turbines to system peaking requirements and emergencies. Turbines, they said, required about four minutes to attain full power output from a cold start while a pumped-storage plant could react in about half that time. Company witnesses also stressed the "spinning reserve" advantages of pumped storage: when in operation the Storm King plant could increase its power output from half to full in ten seconds. While conceding that the output of turbines could be stepped up almost as quickly, Con Edison witnesses claimed that it was more costly to maintain spinning reserve in gas turbines. The complex issue of spinning reserve became more important in the Storm King debate after the power blackout of 1965 which, Con Edison said, would not have been so hard on New Yorkers if the Storm King plant had been operating. Scenic Hudson later countered this charge by arguing that gas turbines would have provided the same insurance and that the causes of Con Edison's blackout problems were more complex than the mere absence of power from Storm King.

In the 1964 hearings, however, the debate over pumped storage versus turbines centered mainly on cost and convenience. Waring capped the Con Edison argument by noting that the Storm King plant would enable the company to retire two old fossil fuel plants in the city, thereby cutting down air pollution. The use of gas turbines as an alternative, he said, would not curb air pollution but would in fact present problems of noise pollution. Doty then pointed out that the sound of gas turbines could be muffled with insulation. He also wondered whether Waring's pure-air claims for the project were realistic inasmuch as the Storm King plant would operate with base power provided by the existing fossil fuel plants in New York.

In the midst of the growing confusion, LeBoeuf cleverly reduced the conflict to one essential theme: the intangible benefits of the scenery versus the measurable benefits of the proposed plant. He tried to underscore this difference in his cross-examination of the elderly Leo Rothschild, whom he cited as the representative of what Scenic Hudson was all about. LeBoeuf barraged Rothschild with questions about his competence to evaluate the plant, his motives, and his lack of understanding of the technical issues. When Rothschild faltered, LeBoeuf concluded with condescension: "Isn't this just one more crusade for you?" Ray Bradford, the village attorney, also took a crack at Rothschild. Noting that the Palisades Park Commission and the Hudson River Conservation Society were neutral on the Storm King issue, Bradford asked Rothschild: "Isn't this organization of yours a last-minute affair to stop the plant?" Of course it was, and having filled in the portrait of Rothschild and the Scenic Hudson organizers as impractical dreamers, Bradford then contrasted them with a man of affairs, Mayor Donohue. In his testimony the mayor played to the audience of building tradesmen by putting some emotion into his script. He talked of the tax benefits the plant would offer and how these added revenues would be used to construct a new village hall, library, garage, recreational center, nature trails, and even a municipal ski slope. His testimony suggested that the new plant would have widespread recreational benefits, although he later admitted privately that he was glad not to be questioned by Doty as to whether anyone outside of Cornwall would use them.

LeBoeuf then took over for a final flourish, bestowing sudden benevolence on those whom he had attempted to destroy in cross-examination. He paid respect to their interest in the scenery. The company, he said, shared that concern. The plant would help the scenery. Cornwall's decrepit waterfront would be cleared of debris, filled in with rock, and turned into a park and visitors center. In the back of the room Bradford and Donohue may have squirmed as LeBoeuf mentioned the park and visitors, but the summary had the desired effect. In June 1964 the FPC hearing examiner approved Con Edison's license.

The examiner's decision concludes the first half of an FPC review. The hearing record and report, together with written comments from the applicant and intervenor, are then forwarded to the full commission, which reviews the proceedings, hears oral arguments, and makes the final decision. Oral arguments on the Storm King case were scheduled for November 17, 1964.

Although Scenic Hudson had scored no points with the FPC, considerable public interest was aroused by the hearings, particularly the melodrama of a writer, an antiques dealer, and an elderly hiker, led by a Spencer Tracy type as their lawyer, taking on a large power company and a government agency. It was not very hard for casual observers to choose sides, even though the bureaucratic largesse of the FPC had made the confrontation possible.

It seems clear, but obviously difficult to prove, that Americans who followed the press coverage took vicarious pleasure in the efforts of Carmer, Frazier, Rothschild, and Doty. By attempting to defend the mountain from the power plant, these four men were waging a symbolic campaign against the onslaught of urbanization, which has affected the lives of most citizens and vastly changed the nation's landscape. Most Americans had never understood or expressed how highly they valued natural beauty until, at places like Storm King, they could see how quickly they were losing it. The organizers of Scenic Hudson were taking a stand that attracted widespread emotional support.

More easily measured was the effect of the FPC hearings in the Hudson Valley, where other residents were encouraged to speak out. In June 1964, when the Hudson River Conservation Society held its annual meeting at the Highland Country Club, president William Osborn unexpectedly faced a membership revolt over his policy of cooperating with Con Edison. When it was revealed that one of Osborn's fellow officers was the mother-in-law of Con Edison's treasurer, several members charged that Con Edison had infiltrated the society. As a result of the meeting, Osborn was forced to poll the membership by mail on the project. By July, with the results in, the society directors reversed themselves by opposing the Storm King project.

In Cornwall the Duggans organized a taxpayer suit against the sale of the village reservoir, and although the suit failed it did solidify the Cornwall opposition and add further to local hostilities. Elsewhere along the river, money and offers of support came into Scenic Hudson. The Storm King plant had become a major issue in the New York metropolitan area.

Taking a dim view of the FPC proceedings were the board members of the Nature Conservancy, who felt, to put it mildly, that director Boardman was leading them astray from the organization's purpose by supporting and funding the legal fight. They also suspected that Boardman was endangering their nonprofit tax status. When the board members forced their director to quit the fight, Boardman left the Nature Conservancy.

The loss of the Nature Conservancy's support prompted Scenic Hudson's organizers to seek assistance from private foundations. But the foundations, which at the time were embarked mainly on poverty programs, seemed uninterested in helping upper-income whites to save a mountain. Significantly, while Scenic Hudson was trying to tap the foundations, Con Edison's president was calling foundation officials to give them a sales talk on the virtues of pumped storage. His message was that if New York's economy was to grow—as the *Daily News, New York Times,* Regional Plan Association, and Mayor Wagner had often said it must—Con Edison needed the plant, and the foundations should not support its opponents. It is difficult to determine whether the phone calls affected the foundations. They do prove, however, that Con Edison had begun to take Scenic Hudson seriously.

Having failed on the foundation trail, Scenic Hudson's leaders decided to take their case to the public and invest the little money they did have to hire a public relations firm. The search led to an organization called Selvage, Lee, and Howard, which describes itself as "concerned with the affairs of industry and government on a national scale." Selvage, Lee, and Howard succeeded in making the battle of Storm King Mountain a national movement.

It is often difficult to determine what public relations firms actually do. About all that can be said of Selvage, Lee, and Howard is that at the time it took on Scenic Hudson's cause it had some fairly conservative clients, including the American Economic Foundation, the American Railway Car Institute, and

Republic Steel. In its public relations campaign for another client, the Portuguese government, the firm had portrayed the 1961 Angolan revolution in Portuguese West Africa as a Kremlin-inspired plot. The campaign was undertaken with some disregard for accuracy as well as taste. Black weeklies, it was charged in a *New Republic* exposé, had been paid to run pictures of mixed couples accompanied by articles describing Portugal's benign racial policies. Other media had received pictures of slain and dismembered Portuguese citizens, together with warnings about the bloodthirsty instincts of the Angolan revolutionaries. "Are they fit to merit the support of the United Nations, or any Christian, civilized society?" asked a handout from Selvage, Lee, and Howard.

A newly arrived executive at the firm, James Cope, played the leading role in taking on the Scenic Hudson account. According to Cope, it was the caliber of Scenic Hudson's membership that made the assignment interesting. He judged that the members were men and women of substance and connections, and that this was one conservation cause that had a chance of succeeding. While Cope is a man who seems drawn to winners, those who have watched his participation sense in him a deeper concern for the beauty of the highlands and for what he regards as Con Edison's shabby corporate performance. Whatever his motivation, Cope, for a fee, became a major force in Scenic Hudson.

Under Cope's direction all the skill and mischief that the firm once turned on Angola was focused on Con Edison. The *Reader's Digest,* which had been good for one story on how Portugal was saving Christianity in Africa, ran a piece on how Scenic Hudson was struggling to preserve natural beauty on the

Hudson. The national and New York media were given background stories on the conflict, which were derived from the research of Cope's assistant, William ("Mike") Kitzmiller, who also became a major behind-the-scenes combatant at Storm King. Kitzmiller discovered that another pumped-storage plant, the Tom Sauk plant in Missouri, had sprung a leak in its upper reservoir. He also uncovered the discomfiting fact that the designer of the Texas Tower, which collapsed, also was responsible for designing the earthen dikes behind Storm King.

Kitzmiller and Cope masterminded an event that dramatically called attention to the struggle. In September 1964 a flotilla of pleasure crafts cruised up the river from Manhattan, with small boats joining the procession from the marinas along the Hudson. The armada surrounded Storm King Mountain in a protest that captured the fancy of the New York press. The organizers were the Duggans of Cornwall and Chauncey Stillman, commodore of the New York Yacht Club. But the idea men were Cope and Kitzmiller.

By October 1964 the two publicists had become the principal legal and political strategists for Scenic Hudson. Doty, whose bills were seldom paid, was quite content to restrict himself to preparing the oral arguments to be presented before the full commission in November. Doty held out little hope that the commission would reverse the hearing examiner's decision, but he worked to lace his brief with legal questions that could become the basis for a court review if the commissioners followed the expected course and Scenic Hudson chose to appeal.

Cope and Kitzmiller, meanwhile, sought to expand the examination of Con Edison's project beyond what they interpreted as the narrow, technical review of the FPC. Through one of Scenic Hudson's backers, they enlisted the help of Republican State Senator R. Watson Pomeroy, who agreed that the New York State Legislative Committee on Natural Resources, which Pomeroy chaired, should hold hearings on the project. Later, in 1965, they also got a boost from Westchester Congressman Richard Ottinger, who helped to arrange congressional hearings on some of the fish and transmission-line issues arising from Con Edison's plans.

Senator Pomeroy's committee held its hearings on the plant at Bear Mountain State Park in November 1964, just two days after the FPC completed its review of the license application. The FPC hearings were disrupted by the appearance of professional pickets, who demonstrated against the plant. Both Cope and Kitzmiller deny that they personally hired the pickets, although it is clear that someone at Selvage and Lee arranged the demonstration, much to the annoyance of Scenic Hudson's citizen supporters and to the anger of the commissioners.

The Bear Mountain hearings went ahead more smoothly and featured the testimony of Alexander Lurkis, who had recently retired as chief engineer of New York City's Bureau of Gas and Electricity. Lurkis attacked Con Edison's pumped-storage plant by making some effusive claims for gas turbines.

Cope had signed up Lurkis as a paid consultant to develop technical arguments in support of Scenic Hudson's claim that gas turbine generators would offer at least the same advantages to Con Edison as a pumped-storage plant. Lurkis told the Pomeroy committee that the turbines would reduce air pollution in New York City, cut electricity charges by $132 million, and prove better for peaking power than the Storm King project. These dramatic assertions were quite a contrast to the more tentative case for gas turbines which Doty had presented to the FPC. Scenic Hudson now seemed to be selling gas turbines rather than merely casting doubts on Con Edison's project.

Lurkis' testimony, which was bitterly disputed by Con Edison engineers, nonetheless had a great impact on the Pomeroy committee as well as on the New York City press. The *Times* included Lurkis' statements in an editorial opposing the plant. Portions of Lurkis' testimony were also included in an eight-page report of the Pomeroy committee. The report, drafted by Kitzmiller, declared the committee opposed to Con Edison's application "until there has been adequate study of the points indicated in this paper."

Another new entry at the Pomeroy hearings was Robert Boyle, a writer for *Sports Illustrated,* who deserves most of the credit for broadcasting the possibility of fishkills at Storm King. Boyle had come to Scenic Hudson's attention through one of his articles, later incorporated in a book, which made the startling point that the Hudson River is the greatest wildlife resource in New York State. Boyle's article noted that there were still millions of fish in the Hudson, despite pollution.

After meeting with Cope and some other Scenic Hudson strategists, Boyle offered to gather all the information he could on fish in the Storm King area of the river. During the FPC hearings Con Edison had routinely produced a fish expert who disclaimed the prospect of fish dangers at the plant site. Boyle talked to marine biologists as well as sports fishermen, who told him that the highlands is a major East Coast spawning ground for anadromous fish—that is, fish who spend their early years in protected waters and then make their way to the sea as adults. Striped bass from the highlands are caught off the coasts of Massachusetts, Rhode Island, Connecticut, Long Island, and New Jersey.

At the Pomeroy hearings Boyle announced his findings. Thousands of young stripers, he said, might be sucked into the Storm King intake tunnel, stored in the upper reservoir, or mangled in the turbine blades. Boyle also revealed that the Department of the Interior and the New York State Conservation Department had expressed written concern to the FPC about the fish dangers. In the back of the hearing room Waring shook his head. He claims that he never knew there was anything still alive in the Hudson.

Boyle's revelations about the fish dangers were dramatically documented in the winter of 1964–1965. With the advent of cold weather the perch, stripers, and other river fish sought out the warm spots of the Hudson: sewer outfalls, industrial waste pipes, and the thermal discharges of power plants, including Con Edison's Nuclear Plant 1 at Indian Point. They jammed beneath the pier, covering the water intakes. Some smaller fish actually swam into the plant; larger ones were crushed in the protective screens.

There had been previous fishkills at Indian Point, but the slaughter of 1964–1965, coming in the midst of the FPC license deliberation, made people in the valley vividly aware of the fact that the river was still alive. That fish were the sacrifices in this awakening is significant. If seals had been killed, the company would have been forced to shut down the plant and would probably have withdrawn its Storm King plans. If the victims had been sharks or rats, Con Edison might have been allowed unlimited power to produce along the river. But in our selective reverence for life, the dead fish were gentle sacrifices, and Con Edison, with an uncanny ability for placing itself in the wrong, was caught slaughtering the symbols of a great awakening.

Boyle, together with other fishermen, formed a new organization, the Hudson River Fishermen's Association, to publicize the Indian Point fishkills and to oppose the Storm King plant. The HRFA is an unusual organization composed of professionals, blue collar workers, scientists, and bureaucrats who have very little in common except their love of sports fishing and their hatred of anyone who slaughters fish in the Hudson. In addition to its fight against Con Edison at Storm King and Indian Point, the HRFA has become a tough strike force against industrial pollution of the river.

In January 1965, on the basis of Boyle's and Lurkis' testimony at Bear Mountain, Doty petitioned the FPC to reopen the hearings so that the fish and turbine issues could be aired more fully. Predictably, the FPC refused, noting that the hearings had dragged on for a year and that nothing would be gained by extending them to discuss issues that the commissioners felt were amply covered in the record. Time was finally running out on Scenic Hudson. If the battle was to be continued, the plant opponents would have to take their campaign to the courts in an appeal of what then seemed to be a certain FPC endorsement of Con Edison's plans. But court appeals are expensive, and although Scenic Hudson was high in enthusiasm it was low on cash.

A critical boost came from Stephan Currier, who ran the Taconic Foundation, a New York-based philanthropy with assets provided by Currier's wife, Audrey, an heir to the estate of financier Andrew Mellon. The small foundation made grants mainly for programs dealing with urban planning and race relations. Currier was drawn to the Storm King fight by a *Newsweek* story on the flotilla of boats that had cruised around the mountain in protest against Con Edison. He asked his friend Lloyd Garrison, a lawyer and member of the Taconic board, to look further into the issue.

Garrison had a fatherlike relationship with the Curriers. They were a young couple, prey to the sharpies who make the foundation rounds the way Jim Fisk once dispensed snake oil. Garrison helped fend off slippery fingers. He also helped in personal ways.

Garrison's compatible liberalism seemed to rest on granite. He was the grandson of William Lloyd Garrison, former dean of the Wisconsin Law School, counsel to Robert Oppenheimer, a leading supporter of Adlai Stevenson's presidential campaigns, and a partner in the New York law firm of Paul, Weiss, Rifkind, Wharton and Garrison.

Garrison spent several weeks with the leaders of Scenic Hudson and concluded that if Currier wanted to aid the cause he could help finance the court appeal. Doty had given the case all the time he could afford. Currier agreed that if the appeal became necessary, he would support it, but only if Garrison accepted the case.

Garrison was tempted, but reluctant, to plunge in. He was drawn to the political dimensions of the case as well as to the scenic issues. The apparent refusal of a bureaucracy to take the protests of citizen groups seriously was a phenomenon he later observed at close hand as president of the New York City School Board under the Lindsay administration. In 1966–68 he presided over the school decentralization program and subsequent crisis, in which neighborhoods tugged for more control while a large school bureaucracy refused to relinquish it. The educators, like the engineers, regarded themselves as the professionals who knew best. Those who presumed to speak for Ocean Hill–Brownsville, Harlem, or in this case Storm King Mountain, were treated by the professionals as representatives of a narrow-interest group.

Perhaps, Garrison felt, the Storm King debate might shed light on the complex issue of public interest and who represented it. But Judge Simon Rifkind, one of his partners, warned that if the FPC approved the license, the chances of an appeal were slim. There would be a lot of effort required, and Garrison, now past the normal retirement age, was trying to cut down his work load.

On March 9, 1965, as Garrison weighed his decision, the FPC commissioners, with one exception, announced theirs. The plant was licensed.

THE TRIAL

Since 1920 the Federal Power Commission had been quietly and routinely licensing private hydroelectric projects on American rivers. Project 2338 had begun as a normal license review, but by 1965 Cornelia Otis Skinner, Brooks Atkinson, James Cagney, Mrs. Fiorello La Guardia, and Pete Seeger were among the celebrities opposing the project at Storm King Mountain. Scenic Hudson had begun as a small group of Hudson Valley citizens who the commission decided, somewhat reluctantly, would be allowed to make comments for the record. By the time of the commission's decision, Scenic Hudson had mushroomed into the vehicle for a national cause. Seldom, if ever, had the FPC been so exposed to the public spotlight.

While the FPC's approval of Con Edison's plan may have seemed like one more impersonal act in a decade of senseless bureaucratic decisions, it was perfectly consistent with what the FPC had always been doing. The bureaucracy had not changed that much; it was the public mood that had altered.

The purpose and priorities of the FPC were those advocated by Governors Smith, Roosevelt, and Lehman, as well as Robert Moses, in their battles with Con Edison in New York State. The FPC was a consumer protection agency established to assure that the private exploitation of rivers was in the public interest, particularly the public interest in reliable, low-cost electrical power.

Congress had instructed the commission to make sure that hydroelectric projects were "adapted to a comprehensive plan for improving or developing a waterway or waterways for the use or benefit of interstate commerce, for the improvement and utilization of water power development, and for other beneficial public uses, including recreation purposes."

FPC employees include many lawyers and engineers, as one might expect in an agency that polices private power production. The specialists give the FPC the technical competence to deal with private utilities. Like other regulatory agencies, the FPC is close to the industry it supervises, a natural tendency in view of the fact that the general public seldom cares about the special issues debated in the hearing room. Job switching between the FPC and the utilities and their representatives is commonplace. Dale Doty, the FPC commissioner turned private utility counsel, is a typical example.

The five commissioners of the FPC, who are presidential appointees, give the agency direction and contribute to its character. The commissioners who reviewed Con Edison's license included some of the most able and independent-minded men ever to serve the agency. One or two of them were unpopular with the more conservative executives of the utility industry. The most controversial commissioner was Charles Ross, a Republican, who came from the Vermont Public Service Commission. Ross was openly critical of some utility companies. His decisions on gas rates severely angered Texas gas and oil producers, who in 1964 pressured President Lyndon Johnson to dump Ross.

Joseph Swidler was the FPC chairman in 1965. In 1970 he was appointed by Nelson Rockefeller to be chairman of the New York State Public Service Commission. Swidler, a Democrat from Chicago, was a political protégé of Adlai Stevenson and had served as general counsel of the Tennessee Valley Authority. President Kennedy's appointment of Swidler to the FPC in 1961 was not a comfortable one and was applauded mainly by those who felt that the FPC had become too friendly toward the utilities during the Eisenhower administration.

The new chairman believed in firm public regulation of the utility industry, and he was guarded when it came to citizen opposition to power plants, particularly from conservationists. His political bias against the protectionist, anti-urban, and usually Republican roots of the conservation movement was reinforced by his legal experience. Lawyers involved in land acquisition programs, as Swidler had been with the TVA, often suspect the motives of those opposing public condemnation of private lands, whether it be for power, urban renewal, or public housing. A lawyer's experience at the settlement table exposes him to people who oppose public programs on democratic grounds and then quietly settle if the negotiated price on their property gets high enough. Acquisition attorneys tend to assume that everyone has his price.

Former FPC colleagues say that in order to understand Swidler's attitude on the Storm King case one must also know something about a concurrent dispute concerning an FPC-licensed ALCOA hydroelectric plant in North Carolina. An enterprising ALCOA executive had left the company to sell sites around the plant's upper reservoir for vacation homes. It was a nice setting for a country place until ALCOA tapped the reservoir for water power. The homes were then left standing around a large mudhole. The homeowners were enraged, ALCOA was on the spot, and the FPC became embroiled in the controversy. The feeling around the agency was that everyone involved was acting selfishly, including the homeowners, who should have known better. The problem was eventually settled when ALCOA agreed to use the reservoir sparingly in the summer months. The ALCOA controversy was, at the time of Storm King, a common reference point at the FPC for defining citizen involvement.

Swidler and some of his fellow commissioners were convinced that Scenic Hudson, like the North Carolina homeowner organization, was a small, temporary pressure group motivated by narrow interest. Viewed from Washington, Scenic Hudson was clearly dwarfed by the larger organizations that originally endorsed the plant. Governor Rockefeller had okayed Con Edison's plans, as had Cornwall officials, labor groups, most state agencies, and the Palisades Interstate Park Commission. Perhaps most significant from the FPC point of view was Laurance Rockefeller's public support of Con Edison in 1964. For most Washington bureaucrats as well as most Americans who have heard of him, Laurance Rockefeller, who directs the Rockefeller family's conservation activities, is one of the nation's leading conservationists. Rockefeller is also a believer in the multiple use of natural resources, and that is how he explained his support for the use of Storm King Mountain as both a power site and an important link in the Palisades Interstate Park system. Finally, from the FPC vantage point there was the significant nonalignment of the Hudson River Conservation Society at the beginning of the Storm King furor.

Swidler and his colleagues rationalized that the FPC had been both patient and indulgent with the property owners around Storm King, who had been allowed, over Con Edison's objections, to intervene in the hearings and then to delay them while Doty prepared a case against the plant. The hearings had dragged on for over a year, more than the average time for a license review. It was time, in March 1965, for the commissioners to make their decision, which hinged on the finding that

> the primary benefit which will be realized from the proposed plant is its economy and reliability as a source of power to meet Con Edison's peaking and emergency requirements. The undisputed proof shows that the Cornwall project would produce savings in the cost of electricity of over $12 million each year as compared with a modern steam plant, the only practical alternative source suggested.

The FPC rejected the alternative of using gas turbines, and judging by its dismissal of any scenic or fish problems, the commission felt that the only real issue in the case was whether there was an alternative. No one, including Scenic Hudson, had argued for no plant at all. The commission concluded:

We have considered with sympathy the protests, which in substance say there must be another source of power as good or better. The record shows, however, that the Cornwall project has large advantages over any other method of meeting the applicant's need for additional peaking power. . . . Here the impact of the project on the surrounding area is minimal while the need for electricity from this economical and dependable source is great.

Charles Ross, the maverick from Vermont, dissented. He recalls that his position was based on the way the commission had treated Scenic Hudson and had reached its decision, not on the merits of the plant. Ross feels that his colleagues, by assuming that the opponents were merely a group of angry property owners, had misread their motives. Ross sensed that during the hearings the plant had become a matter of concern throughout the valley and was being questioned by many people whose only interest was the beauty of the Hudson Highlands. The FPC, Ross says, owed this interest more than indulgence, and at the very least the agency should have held hearings in the New York City area—a suggestion that had been made by Doty but resisted by the FPC. Rather than being suspicious of Scenic Hudson, Ross claims, the FPC should have fully investigated the questions it raised. Too great a burden was placed on citizens to prove their allegations about fish dangers and turbine alternatives. He also feels that the commission was too ready to credit Con Edison's case. One example was Con Edison's rejection of the possibility of burying most of the transmission lines, not just those over the river. LeBoeuf and Waring had argued that it was prohibitively expensive to bury the lines and that its city customers "should not be saddled with these exorbitant costs to satisfy the sensibilities of a few estate holders." Yet, Ross said in his dissenting opinion, the company's estimates were based on New York City excavation costs, not those, say, of burying the lines along the Penn Central's right of way to New York. Ross noted that the company and the FPC agreed that pumped storage was economically superior to other means of power production. Why then could not some of the savings be invested in additional underground transmission lines?

But Ross' major point was that the Storm King hearings produced questions that the FPC should have answered fully. It was the agency's job to remove all doubts, especially because, as Ross put it in his dissent, "had this area of the 'Hudson Highlands' been declared a state or national park, that is, had the people in the area already spoken, we probably would have listened and might well have refused to license it."

Ross' dissent to the commission's ruling represented an important hook on which Scenic Hudson could hang a court appeal, and it was a major factor in Lloyd Garrison's decision to take on the case. The wheels began turning in April, when Doty prepared a formal application to the FPC to reconsider. It was purely an automatic step, and Doty's last major contribution. The FPC turned down the request and the path was now open to the federal appeals court. Garrison, Con Edison, and the FPC began mapping out their briefs.

Garrison's law firm was all eminence but offered very little experience when it came to the specialized administrative law of the FPC. A number of lawyers worked on the Scenic Hudson brief, including Judge Simon Rifkind and Edward Costikyan, who were among Garrison's partners. Charles Reich, who in 1965 was known only as a specialist in administrative law at the Yale Law School and not as the author of *The Greening of America,* lent his advice, as did Whitney North Seymour, a friend of the Duggans who later became the U.S. District Attorney for Southern New York State. A number of recent Yale and Harvard law graduates did the legwork. The most important among them was a Harvard graduate named Albert Butzel.

Butzel is an excellent representative of the young people who began fighting the Storm King plant in 1965. His only experience in the conservation movement had been filling the bird feeder in his suburban Detroit home. Like other young aides joining the struggle, such as Kitzmiller or Nancy Mathews of the Sierra Club, Butzel might have been more comfortable if the protectors of Storm King Mountain had been low-income blacks.

Now that Scenic Hudson had grown from a living room discussion group into a movement served by publicists, lawyers, fund raisers, and national celebrities, it also manifested the inner conflicts of a large organization. The young, liberal Butzel, for instance, was quite a contrast to the older, conservative Cope. Dissension did in fact break out when folk singer Pete Seeger joined the camp with plans to build the *Clearwater,* a replica of a Hudson River sloop, from which he later gave concerts at riverside towns in support of Storm King and other river causes. Carl Carmer echoed the sentiments of some of Scenic Hudson's conservative supporters when he bitterly denounced Seeger's participation. Carmer's position was based not only on Seeger's politics but on a personal disagreement with the folksinger over his use in 1947 of Carmer's endorsement of the *People's Song Book,* which, Carmer claimed, almost got him blacklisted.

Opposition to Con Edison's plans proved to be stronger

than Scenic Hudson's inner conflicts, which were seldom publicized. Butzel's legal skills endeared him to Scenic Hudson's organizers, who became far less interested in his political opinions than impressed by his ability to challenge Con Edison. It is also interesting to note that Waring developed a respect for Butzel, which was reciprocated, when the two men debated the virtues of gas turbines during subsequent FPC hearings. But that was later on, after Butzel became Garrison's principal assistant. In 1965 he was just one of many young lawyers running errands and stabbing into the darkness of the FPC's administrative laws.

As Judge Rifkind had warned, the history of court intrusions into the legal domain of the regulatory agencies was not encouraging. Because of the technical complexity of most of the agencies' cases plus, of course, the traditional separation of judicial and executive powers, judges seldom second-guess the regulators. About the most an aggrieved party can hope for is a court ruling instructing an agency to reconsider its decision.

Generally speaking, there are two main arguments that may prompt a judge to remand an FPC decision. The first is that the agency has not compiled a sufficient record and lacks substantial evidence to support its decision. Garrison and his numerous advisers and workers used the fish dangers, Lurkis' testimony about gas turbines, and the findings of the Pomeroy committee to build a string of questions about the plant and to raise doubts about whether the FPC had really answered them. The second major argument against an FPC decision is that it violates the congressional mandate of the Federal Power Act and its subsequent amendments. Here the Scenic Hudson brief argued that the Storm King plant did not conform to the comprehensive plan and "beneficial public uses" sections of the act.

Scenic Hudson pointed out that a second planned pumped-storage plant across the river at Breakneck Ridge had not figured in the Storm King hearings. The brief also drew on every case it could find, including Doty's 1953 Namekagon decision, to suggest that the commission be required to consider scenic and historic values as a "beneficial public use" to which a licensed plant must conform under the Federal Power Act. These two arguments were tightly woven to form a modest request of the court: send the Con Edison license back to the FPC for further hearings.

Garrison, after reviewing his brief, concluded that the chances of the appeal were quite slim. "About 10 percent, at best," is how he estimated it to the Scenic Hudson board members. The 10 percent, Garrison now says, was based partly on the choice of the Second Circuit Court to hear the appeal. He hoped that some of the judges in the circuit, which includes the Hudson Valley, might have a special affection for the highlands.

The reason for the pessimism, aside from the traditional reluctance of courts to remand FPC decisions, may have been that the brief did not have very much going for it. With the exception of Ross' dissent, the charge that the FPC had not built an adequate record for its decision rested mainly on Scenic Hudson-inspired evidence, such as the paid-for claims of Lurkis, the Kitzmiller-drafted findings of the Pomeroy committee, and the Boyle-researched fish dangers. In other words, the FPC had answered to its satisfaction the usual agency questions about the plant. What it had not done was to answer those raised by Scenic Hudson to Scenic Hudson's satisfaction.

The brief was also adventurous in its interpretation of Congress' intent under the Federal Power Act. The idea that hydroelectric plants must serve the public interest in scenery as well as the need for power was hard to document. In fact, the legislative history of the act and its amendments and the prior license approvals of the FPC suggest that in licensing the plant the agency was probably doing just what La Follette, Norris, and Roosevelt had in mind: making an engineering decision in line with the public interest in low-cost electricity. The Namekagon decision of 1953 had firmly established recreation as a "beneficial public use," but the notion that scenery fell into that category rested less on legal statements or precedents than on the hope that natural beauty and a concern for the environment were ideas whose time had come in a maturing American society.

Judge Rifkind, Garrison's partner, also sensed that the legal arguments alone would not work. He encouraged his colleagues to stress the importance of natural beauty in the early part of the brief, thus introducing the legal arguments by underlining the unique scenic value of the resource. Some of the drafters resisted, arguing that an emphasis on the soft issue of natural beauty was a risky tactic. Rifkind replied that if the court was to be persuaded, the judges would have to share the perception that this was not just another squabble over a power site to be settled by the customary review of appropriate law. Garrison agreed, revised the brief accordingly, and dispatched it to the Second Circuit Court in August 1965.

The briefs from the FPC and Con Edison were much larger than Scenic Hudson's. They seemed like tanks, wheeled into the Second Circuit's Foley Square courthouse to blow the Garrison brief into the streets of lower Manhattan.

"The evidence supporting the plant," said the company

brief prepared by Randall LeBoeuf and his associates, is "not merely substantial, it is overwhelming." The company reviewed the importance of the project, praised the wisdom of the FPC in licensing it, and attacked Scenic Hudson. In demeaning but prophetic passages the company charged that "the petitioners have no real hope of persuading the commission to reverse its findings on issues fully and carefully considered, and merely seek to kill the project by a war of attrition." The company lawyers barely concealed their contempt for the "eminent Mr. Lurkis," the "alleged expert" whose testimony Scenic Hudson hoped to use in more hearings. "For this court to remand on such a showing," said Consolidated Edison, "would make ludicrous the entire administrative process."

The FPC brief was a tour de force weighted with ninety-eight citations, including seventy-four cases, eleven laws, twelve books, and the U.S. Constitution, to justify the license decision, and it left the reader with the impression that the commission had been aggrieved by Scenic Hudson. "Petitioners," said the FPC, "did not come near to presenting legally sufficient evidence in support of their positions. . . . They now seek to have this court hold that the commission was required to supply their deficiencies, and should have developed and presented evidence on points as to which the commission felt no lack."

The commission then moved to a fundamental conflict: Who represented the public interest, Scenic Hudson or the FPC? In his brief Garrison cast Scenic Hudson as a representative of the "unorganized public." "The pattern of federal administrative law," replied the FPC, "would be seriously undermined if any interested person or group were permitted to undertake the role of representative of the public interest in the courts."

That role "Congress has ascribed to the commission under the Federal Power Act."

The commission said that it did not regard itself as an adversary in the license application. Rather its established function was to hear the evidence of special interests, such as Scenic Hudson and Consolidated Edison, and then on the basis of its experience and the expertise of its staff to judge how the "public interest" would best be served. Scenic Hudson had not made a case against the plant, argued the commission, partly because it had no economic interest motivating it. Now, having failed as an intervenor, continued the FPC, Scenic Hudson was casting itself as a representative of the public, but it could not have it both ways. It lacked the legal standing to appeal the license decision because it was not an "aggrieved party," and only parties with an economic stake are entitled to judicial review under the Federal Power Act. If Scenic Hudson was an "aggrieved party," concluded the commission, it had the responsibility to prove its case against the plant and not expect that job to be done by the FPC.

Randall LeBoeuf was displeased. He did not wish his client's case to be entangled in what amounted to a jurisdictional dispute between Scenic Hudson and the FPC over who represented the public interest. Consolidated Edison simply wanted to build a power plant. LeBoeuf urged the FPC lawyers to stick to the merits of the commission's decision. Richard Solomon, the FPC general counsel, resisted, claiming that a basic tenet of administrative law would be undermined if any group suddenly announced it was speaking for the public interest. If Scenic Hudson succeeded, argued the FPC, "literally thousands" would be encouraged to intervene in hearings, seek court reviews, and disrupt future proceedings. The integrity of the FPC was at stake, as were the nation's long-range power needs.

The briefs were argued before Judges Waterman, Hays, and Lumbard of the Second Circuit Court on October 8, 1965. Oral arguments are crucial. They give the judges, who have copies of the briefs before them, a chance to examine who the drafters are and, during questioning, to determine what is important to them. Garrison made it clear that the mountain was foremost in his mind. He avoided a detailed summary of his arguments and gave what even Waring of Con Edison, who attended the proceedings, regards as an eloquent statement of the beauty and importance of Storm King. Randall LeBoeuf followed and was brisk and impressive. Then came Josephine Klein, an FPC attorney, who presented the case of the commission. That a woman should argue on behalf of their plant was a novel and unsettling experience for Con Edison's executives, some of whom claim that she sabotaged the plant. Miss Klein's presentation suffered from the length of the FPC brief and a few sharp questions from Judge Lumbard, who at one point asked: "Does the FPC really contend that Storm King will look better with the plant?"

The judges weighed their decision in November and early December of 1965. According to the legal legends of the case, their opinion was actually written by candlelight during the November 9 blackout of the northeast, which made the outcome even more uncertain. On December 29, 1965, a reporter for *The New York Times* was the first to learn of their decision and he relayed it to the attorneys.

The lawyers for Con Edison and the FPC knew they were in trouble as soon as they heard the opening lines of the decision. The judges quoted "the great German traveler Baedeker," who called the Hudson "finer than the Rhine." It seemed, said one Con Edison attorney, that the judges were about to break into song. The court agreed with Scenic Hudson that the "unique beauty and historic significance" of the Storm King area had to be taken into consideration by the FPC. The FPC, said the court, "must include as a basic concern the preservation of natural beauty and of national historic shrines, keeping in mind that, in our affluent society, the cost of a project is only one of several factors to be considered."

The judges not only confirmed the value of scenic beauty; they also ruled that Scenic Hudson had the legal standing to assure that "the Federal Power Commission will adequately protect the public interest in the aesthetic, conservational, and recreational aspects of power development." Virtually every challenge the FPC lawyers made against Scenic Hudson's standing was thrown back at them. On the point that the appeal could encourage intervention from "ad hoc" citizen groups in other license hearings, the court ruled just the opposite, that Scenic Hudson was actually expediting the administrative process by consolidating opponents into one organization and one appeal. Ironically, the court also held that the FPC's original agreement, over Con Edison's objection, to allow Scenic Hudson's intervention in the case added further legitimacy to Scenic Hudson's legal standing in appealing the ruling.

The judges also concurred with Scenic Hudson's claim, as well as with Ross' assertion in his dissent, that the FPC had not compiled an adequate hearing record. "Especially in a case of this type," said the court, "where public interest and concern is so great, the commission's refusal to receive the Lurkis testimony, as well as the proffered information on fish protection devices and underground transmission facilities, exhibits a disregard of the statute and of judicial mandates instructing the commission to probe all feasible alternatives."

Finally, the judges dismissed the FPC argument that Scenic Hudson could not impose upon the commission the obligations to prove or disprove its allegations about the plant. The judges quoted from Commissioner Ross' dissent:

> *The thread running through this case is that the applicant is entitled to a license upon making a prima facie case. My own personal regulatory philosophy compels me to reject this approach. This commission, of its own motion, should always seek to insure that a full and adequate record is presented to it. A regulatory commission can insure continuing confidence in its decisions only when it has used its staff and its own expertise in a manner not possible for the uninformed and poorly financed public. With our intimate knowledge of other systems and to a lesser degree of their plans, it should be possible to resolve all doubts as to alternative sources. This may have been done, but the record does not speak. Let it do so.*

The court then reminded the FPC of its planning responsibilities. The Congress, said the court, has instructed the FPC to gauge "the totality of a project's immediate and long-range effects, and not merely the engineering and navigational aspects." Then, in the most often quoted section of their ruling, the judges said:

> *In this case, as in many others, the commission has claimed to be the representative of the public interest. This role does not permit it to act as an umpire blandly calling balls*

*and strikes for adversaries appearing before it; the right of
the public must receive active and affirmative protection at
the hands of the commission.*

The decision was a serious defeat for Con Edison, a rude
shock for the FPC, and a resounding victory for Scenic Hudson,
which, starting with a group of frustrated citizens, had developed
sufficient strength to block a major power plant against the
pressure of two formidable bureaucracies. That was an unheard-
of accomplishment.

The federal court ruling meant that the FPC would have
to study and hold hearings on the plant all over again. At the
very least the project would be delayed for two years or more.
Randall LeBoeuf immediately requested a Supreme Court review. But FPC lawyers, not anxious to have the Warren court
deal with the question of agency responsibility, reported to the
high court that the commission, in effect, could live with the appeals court decision. In May 1966 the Supreme Court refused to
hear the case, and the Scenic Hudson decision became a legal
milestone with repercussions that extended far beyond FPC law
and the fate of Storm King Mountain.

By ruling that a conservation organization could sue to
protect the public interest in the environment under the Federal
Power Act, the Second Circuit Court encouraged citizen suits
against the actions of other federal agencies. The Federal Communications Commission and the Department of Transportation
were among the first agencies affected, and the issues were not
just environmental. In *Office of Communication of United
Church of Christ* v. *FCC* (1966), Chief Justice Warren Burger,
then a judge in the District Circuit, was apparently reacting di-

rectly to the Scenic Hudson decision when he ruled that the church group could intervene in a license proceeding before the FCC. Judge Burger said that it was desirable to have "audience participation" in FCC hearings, and that "consumers are generally among the best vindicators of the public interest."

The citizen suits presented problems for the courts, including the need to separate the new-style public interest advocates from the old-line crackpots. Justice Burger referred to this problem in his United Church of Christ opinion, concluding that perhaps the sincerity of a citizen group is best determined by its willingness "to shoulder the burdensome and costly process of intervention."

In 1969 Congress offered some help to the courts with its passage of the National Environmental Policy Act. The act, which became effective on January 1, 1970, states the public interest in the environment and mandates all federal agencies to consider the environmental consequences of their decisions. Conservation lawyers regard the National Environmental Policy Act as an extension of the federal court ruling that environmental factors must be considered under the Federal Power Act. In 1970 the right of citizen groups to use federal courts to protect the public's new environmental interests received an important clarification in the Hudson River Expressway cases, then was thrown into some confusion in the Mineral King case, both of which are discussed in a later chapter.

The political impact of the Scenic Hudson decision was just as important as the legal consequences. By giving Scenic Hudson and other citizen groups new power in dealing with the agencies of the Hudson River and by delaying the Storm King plant, the Second Circuit Court created a temporary political vacuum. While the court had made it clear that the old methods of carving up the Hudson's resources were no longer acceptable, it was uncertain what new arrangements would take their place and under whose control. Those questions were answered in the years immediately following the 1965 decision, a period of intense maneuvering that is best introduced through the activities of Governor Nelson Rockefeller.

POLITICS

New York voters had turned to Nelson Rockefeller to revive the state economy in the 1958 recession. He responded with a public construction program far more ambitious than that of any previous Governor, save DeWitt Clinton. Billions were invested in new roads. A new state university system and a vast state office complex in Albany were constructed.

Rockefeller's building programs helped revive the state's economy by creating thousands of new jobs. But his emphasis on development programs came from his heritage, not from the political needs of the moment. "Father was a development man," recalled the Governor in a recent book correcting the popular impression that John D. Rockefeller, Jr., was strictly a philanthropist. While the elder Rockefeller did dispense millions on worthy causes, he also built Rockefeller Center, the roads in Arcadia National Park, and the Cloisters on the Hudson, to name but a few projects. The Governor was a builder because he was a Rockefeller.

Con Edison's Storm King project had struck his fancy. It was a bold engineering challenge and, as he was told in an early briefing, it would keep New York City's economy growing. But after his original endorsement, Rockefeller paid little attention to the project. His mind was on other matters, including the Republican presidential nomination.

When Rockefeller returned to New York after delivering a bristling attack against Goldwater supporters at the San Francisco convention of 1964, he discovered that the project was becoming a major state issue. In the fall he watched the issue turn against him and his brother Laurance. Laurance Rockefeller was being singled out for his role in the transmission line negotiations and his subsequent support of Con Edison. The Governor was criticized for his silence.

Leading the attack was Richard Ottinger, a Democratic Congressman from a Westchester County district that included Pocantico Hills, the Rockefeller estate in North Tarrytown. Ottinger's election to Congress in 1964 was an indication of the growing public interest in the plant controversy and the Hudson River. The district was traditionally Republican, and its Democratic candidates were often regarded as sacrifices rather than aspirants. The former New Frontiersman upset the pattern by embracing the Hudson while making pollution, power lines, and Con Edison his principal opponents. He added Nelson Rockefeller to the list after his election.

Ambition and wealth were two qualities that Ottinger and Rockefeller shared. Ironically enough, they also both had uncles with close ties to Con Edison's past. William Rockefeller, the Governor's great-uncle, was a founder of the Consolidated Gas Company. Ottinger's uncle was a company ally in the state legislature during the Smith and Roosevelt administrations and he had run against Smith's and Roosevelt's public power policies in 1928, narrowly losing his bid for Governor to Roosevelt and perhaps altering the future course of American politics.

Ottinger's attacks on the Rockefeller administration disturbed the Governor because the freshman Congressman was skillful in getting publicity, particularly through the use of congressional hearings. One possible reason for the Congressman's success was the presence on his staff of William Kitzmiller, the Cope protégé who left the public relations firm of Selvage and Lee to join Ottinger during his first term. By 1970, when Ottinger relinquished his House seat to run unsuccessfully for the Senate, he had averaged a hearing a year on Hudson River subjects ranging from fish to transmission lines to scenery. A recurring note in these hearings was the revelation of some fact or incident damaging to Nelson Rockefeller, to which the Governor usually responded with a thunderously announced new state program for the Hudson.

Ottinger opened his attack with a hearing in May 1965 on Hudson River fish, in which he publicized the fact that although the Governor supported Con Edison, the New York State Conservation Department had serious doubts about the effectiveness of the fish protection screens the company proposed for the Storm King plant. New York Senator Robert Kennedy appeared at the hearing to announce his support for the striped bass of the Hudson. His interest and expertise, he pointed out, were based on the fact that although the stripers were born in New York, they were caught off Massachusetts.

Ottinger maneuvered the fish hearings by enlisting the aid of Congressman T. A. Thompson of Louisiana, chairman of the House Subcommittee on Fisheries and Wildlife Conservation. Ottinger learned that Thompson had a special fondness for anadromous fish, and that while Thompson's bill proposing research on anadromous species was languishing in the Senate he was ready to turn loose his subcommittee. Ottinger pointed out that anadromous fish were a project issue at Storm King and suggested that the subcommittee avail itself of the publicity by holding hearings of its own.

The Thompson subcommittee hearings offered a platform for the vast network of sports fishing organizations to present their views on the Storm King project. The Fishing Bugs, Surf and Stream Anglers, Striped Bass Committee of the Long Island League of Salt Water Sportsmen, Stripers Unlimited, and Sportsmen's Council of the Marine District of New York State were among the organizations that expressed strong, often emotional opposition. The hearings also gave Scenic Hudson's lawyers the opportunity to incorporate congressional concern for the Storm King project in the brief they were preparing for the appeals court review in October 1965.

Governor Rockefeller's first public effort to blunt the charges of his critics and to seize the initiative came in March 1965 when he announced the formation of a study committee on the Hudson. Study committees are a well-worn political device, and the Hudson has had its share. In 1939, for example, Governor Herbert Lehman appointed a committee to examine the water pollution problem, which was then a matter of some concern. Lehman's committee reported that the state was doing an effective job, that by 1940 all the towns in the valley would be under orders to clean their wastes, and that with "scientific planning" most of the river's problems could be corrected.

Rockefeller's 1965 committee, called the Hudson River Valley Commission, was distinguished by the caliber and diversity of its membership, which included former Governor Averell Harriman, Lowell Thomas, Marian Sulzberger Heiskill, author William H. Whyte, and the presidents of Vassar College, IBM, and the Albany bank in which most of the state's funds are deposited. The chairman of the commission was Laurance Rockefeller.

The Governor gave the Hudson River Valley Commission a brisk send-off. Rather than merely launch it by an executive order, he sent a bill to the state legislature asking for confirmation of his appointments and support of the commission's purpose. In his accompanying message Rockefeller noted that by the 1966 session of the legislature the commission would prepare and present a program for the "protection, improvement, and desirable development" of the Hudson. Rockefeller stressed that "this will be a New York State program as part of its proper responsibilities under our federal system of government." The message was clear: Rockefeller was acknowledging that Storm King raised questions about the future of the Hudson River, but the Rockefeller administration was going to deal with them without federal intervention.

To demonstrate New York's commitment the Governor

also announced a billion-dollar program to clean up the waters of the Hudson and other state rivers. The so-called pure waters program was an unprecedented state antipollution measure and was made even more startling by the enthusiasm with which voters endorsed it in the fall elections of 1965. The pure waters bond referendum passed with a four-to-one majority, one of the most impressive victories in the history of state politics.

Despite the vigor of the Governor's response, Congressman Ottinger continued his attack with the introduction of a bill in the spring of 1965 establishing the Hudson Highlands as a national scenic riverway. Ottinger's bill proposed that the river and a mile-wide strip of land on each side of it from Yonkers to Newburgh be placed under the jurisdiction of the Department of the Interior, whose Secretary would be authorized to prepare a recreation-and-park plan for the wide sweep of riverway, to acquire up to 5,000 acres of land along it, and to license future uses of then vacant shoreline. Such a bold program, with its implied attack on New York's ability to deal effectively with river problems, might have gone unnoticed had it not been for the agreement of Alaska Congressman Ralph Rivers, chairman of the House Subcommittee on National Parks and Recreation, and ranking committee Democrat Leo O'Brien from Albany to hold hearings on the bill in the Hudson Valley. With this development twelve other New Jersey and New York Congressmen submitted similar or identical pieces of legislation.

Ottinger's counterattack is explained by a little-noticed controversy that was developing in his district early in 1965 concerning a rumored expressway that the state was planning to build along the east bank of the river from Croton-on-Hudson to New York City. The expressway, which became public knowledge in the summer of 1965, was to be built partly on landfill in the Tappan Zee section of the river. Conservation organizations, including most of those backing Scenic Hudson, recognized that the expressway presented scenic and aquatic disruptions at least as substantial as those of the Storm King project. As we shall see in the next chapter, the expressway eventually replaced Storm King as the principal *cause célèbre* of Hudson Valley residents. But in 1965 the public's attention was drawn mainly to the struggle over the mountain, except in Ottinger's district, where concern over the new road was growing. For Ottinger and his conservation supporters the concern centered on Nelson and Laurance Rockefeller's personal involvement in the planning of the new expressway. In other words, the two state leaders, who had seemed unreliable or disinterested during the Storm King fracas, were now developing an equally damaging expressway project. To the conservationists and Ottinger, the Rockefellers' professed interest in the river's ecology seemed to be a sham.

The congressional hearings on Ottinger's bill began in July 1965 in the Westchester city of Yonkers, which borders on the river. Ottinger opened the proceedings with the announcement, delivered with persuasive innocence, that he had been unable to get the Governor's assistance in planning the federal takeover of the Hudson. Rockefeller's Hudson River Valley Commission, meanwhile, had hired staff members, leased offices on Iona Island in the highlands, and opened hearings of its own.

The Yonkers hearings provided the first forum for the mayors of the Hudson to express their thoughts on the future of the river in light of the issues raised at Storm King. The mayors, often accompanied by representatives from local chambers of commerce and union organizations, said that they appreciated the scenery as much as anyone but that, like Governor Rockefeller, they were not about to release any of their control over land use to a higher level of government. Some of the mayors felt that programs of public acquisition for recreation and open space were socialistic. All of them made it clear that these land acquisition programs were unresponsive to their desperate need for tax-producing industry.

The suspicions of local officials were further aroused in the fall of 1965 when a third investigative body arrived in the valley. The new task force had been dispatched by Stewart Udall, Secretary of the Interior. Udall found himself in the middle of exchanges between David and Goliath. He was a friend of Ottinger and respectful of Rockefeller. Nothing would have pleased him more than expanding his department's responsibilities beyond the Roosevelt-Vanderbilt historical sites in Hyde Park. But the Hudson was Rockefeller country, and a Secretary of the Interior does not take the family lightly. The Rockefellers have donated many of the nation's parks, and Laurance Rockefeller is associated with or directs seven public and private agencies that do business with the department. Laurance Rockefeller's conservation interests are so vast that they have recently become the focus of a report, circulated within the Department of the Interior and of unknown authorship, citing in tones reminiscent of an FBI dossier two conservation organizations that he "controls," eleven that he has "infiltrated," and eight that are "suspect." Secretary Udall directed his task force to cooperate with both the Rockefeller commission and the congressional committee. He also appointed the study group to give him an independent appraisal of the proper federal role in future Hudson River programs.

The Hudson River Valley Commission published its findings in February 1966. The report gave top priority to the immediate public acquisition of 20,000 acres of open land along the river and proposed the establishment of scenic and historic corridors joining the existing park holdings, including a series of waterside parks that would allow the public greater access to the river.

The Rockefeller group also called attention to the recently approved pure waters program and predicted that while the clean-up campaign for the river would be difficult, the problem of water pollution had to be solved so that swimming and other "water contact" sports could be introduced along the river.

The commission's report did not restrict itself to scenic, conservation, and recreational recommendations, but also called for the extensive redevelopment of industrial sites along the Hudson and for the provision of waterside housing, marinas, and parks. To accomplish these goals the commission recommended a combination of urban renewal, open space, park, transportation, and water-pollution control programs; and it candidly acknowledged that the state of New York, acting alone, could not pull it off.

Surveying the vast spectrum of local, state, and federal bureaucracies with responsibilities on the river—these include, in addition to the numerous local jurisdictions, seventeen different state and federal agencies employing close to a million people —the report concluded that informal agreements, coordination, and executive orders would not do. A federal-state compact agency with power to force cooperative action and to veto harmful projects was, in the judgment of the commission, the only answer.

This proposal pushed the Rockefeller administration beyond the scope and intent of Ottinger's legislation. The commission's recommendations encompassed not just one stretch of the river but the entire Hudson and the Mohawk River as well. But the commission's report also contained some stringent conditions. The compact agency was to have fifteen members. Because most of the area to be covered was within New York State, the commission argued, the Governor should have nine appointees. New Jersey's brief stretch entitled it to three, and the federal government would get the remaining three appointees.

The Department of the Interior issued its findings in August 1966. The report covered much of the same material as the Rockefeller study but disagreed with a few important recommendations, including the proposed fifteen-member commission. It should be a simple three-man commission, the report said, with one appointee from each state and one from the federal government. New Jersey's Governor Richard Hughes agreed.

In anticipation that a compromise might be worked out, and in response to a bill submitted by Congressman Ottinger and supported by Udall, Congress passed the Hudson River Compact Law in September 1966. The law gave the Secretary of the Interior review power over all federally related projects along the Hudson for three years or until the appointee issue could be resolved and the compact agency approved by the legislatures of New York and New Jersey and then ratified by Congress. By the September 1969 deadline, Governor Rockefeller's position on New York's majority interest in the river remained unchanged. The law was extended for another three years.

The impasse over the compact agency was often blamed on

Governor Rockefeller's stubborn refusal to give up power. To be sure, he seemed unreasonably adamant about retaining control of the Hudson. But the problems of the river, as they were highlighted at Storm King, stemmed less from the structural arrangement of river agencies than from the agencies' individual performance and motivation. The compact idea has become a standard solution for a situation of jurisdictional conflict; and although a myriad of agencies and local jurisdictions are represented on the Hudson, Storm King raised more questions about what they were or were not doing than about how they were relating.

For all its merits, a compact places one large bureaucratic layer over many smaller ones. The impact on the quality of performance is debatable. Presumably, a compact introduces the superior resources of the federal government into a regional problem. Yet, if state and local performance on the river was bad, the federal government's record was even worse, especially from an environmentalist's point of view.

If one opposed Con Edison's Storm King plant, the immediate enemy was the federal agency that licensed it, the FPC. The same held true for Con Edison's proliferating nuclear plants at Indian Point, which were authorized by the AEC. The public agency with the most sweeping powers over water pollution is the U.S. Army Corps of Engineers, another federal agency. In 1888 and 1899 the corps was authorized to enforce two federal laws prohibiting the discharge of all but municipal wastes into navigable rivers and providing criminal penalties for violators. One of these laws was designed specifically to curb discharges into the Hudson River and New York Harbor. Not until 1963 did the corps enforce the laws against industrial polluters. That year the corps ordered such large corporations as Standard

Brands in Peekskill and General Motors in Tarrytown to stop dumping their wastes—yeast and toilet water in the case of Standard Brands and paint residues in the case of General Motors—into the Hudson. The two companies, among many others, continued to dump.

In 1970 the U.S. Attorney's Office in New York City, staffed with some able and politically ambitious appointees, pioneered the use of the refuse acts to press criminal charges against Hudson River polluters. Standard Brands was fined $125,000 and General Motors was subpoenaed before a grand jury, where Assistant District Attorney John Burns III pressed for a criminal indictment. Just as the stiff enforcement procedures were beginning to have an effect, U.S. Attorney General John Mitchell warned the New York office that its antipollution campaign seemed more like a vendetta than a quest for clean water. Mitchell's aides interceded in the General Motors controversy and Burns was taken off the case. Burns got angry and was fired for leaking details of the General Motors prosecution to the press. Burns denied that he talked to the press and claimed that he was fired because the federal government was not taking the antipollution campaign seriously.

The federal government's antipollution program was clearly ineffective at its own Hudson River facilities. The West Point Military Academy and the Watervliet Arsenal, both federal installations, were among the river's most persistent and intransigent polluters. The government was also a weak partner in the financing of sewage treatment plants and other projects of the pure waters program. By 1970 the federal cash contribution to the $.7 billion committed in state and local funds was only $44 million.

While Congress and the various Hudson River study committees pondered the complexities of the federal system and debated the merits of compact agencies, the protagonists in the Storm King dispute were reacting to the new interest in the river with programs, commitments, and maneuvers of immediate consequence.

As some of Scenic Hudson's organizers had prophesied, Con Edison's plans had precipitated the possibility of further industrial development in the highlands. In 1965 the Georgia Pacific Company announced that it would build a plywood plant at Little Stony Point. Governor Rockefeller interceded privately and persuaded company officials to drop the idea, promising to find them another location on the river. That site turned out to be in Buchanan, where Mayor Burke, the valley's foremost collector of tax producers, tucked the factory next to one of Con Edison's nuclear plants.

The Governor and his brother also approached executives of Central Hudson Gas and Electric in an effort to persuade them to drop their option to Breakneck Ridge, where the company planned to build a pumped-storage plant. The executives acceded to the Rockefellers' request, persuaded no doubt by the problems Con Edison faced across the gorge. Breakneck Ridge was purchased by a Rockefeller family enterprise, Jackson Hole Preserve, Inc., which later turned it over to the state as a public park. Central Hudson emerged from the transaction with a statesmanlike image and tried to build on its new good will by financing a private planning agency to establish development goals for the mid-Hudson region.

Meanwhile, in November 1966, the FPC had resumed its hearings on the Con Edison project in Washington. This time the case against the plant was presented by Garrison, who led a trio of lawyers on behalf of Scenic Hudson, and David Sive, who represented the Sierra Club. The appealing underdog quality of Scenic Hudson's opposition in the first hearing gave way to elaborate technical arguments and often brisk cross-examination of Con Edison witnesses. Popular interest in the controversy waned as the hearings dragged on through the spring. They were concluded in May 1967, only to be reopened again in the fall when the Connecticut Board of Fisheries asked to intervene.

There was little drama in the proceedings. Each side seemed merely to be building a case for an inevitable second court appeal, and the hearing examiners' decision in support of the plant in August 1968 was hardly a shock. Three months later New York City unexpectedly asked to intervene. James Marcus had resigned as Water Commissioner, and New York now opposed the project because of its proximity to the Moodna Tunnel. More hearings were held.

New York City's objection was based on a new plant design in which Con Edison proposed to bury its powerhouse. The deeper excavation meant that rock blasting and digging would take place even closer to the tunnel. Ironically, the burial of the powerhouse was in part a concession by Con Edison to the scenic objections against the plant. The unforeseen result of New York's intervention was symptomatic. Nothing that Con Edison did seemed to turn out right. The drama of Storm King was no longer played out in the FPC hearing room or in court; the controversy now centered on the crisis that developed within the company itself.

Burying the plant was only one concession that backfired. Another was an offer by Con Edison to undertake a $175,000 study of the Hudson River fish, which the company hoped would win it some friends but which ended up only increasing its enemies. The study was conducted by a private firm with a review board composed of federal and state officials, but not one representative of a conservation organization. The Hudson River Fishermen's Association led the opposition, charging that the study was therefore suspect; the accusation gained support when the study group concluded that the Storm King project would inflict negligible damage on aquatic life.

Con Edison's problems, of course, went deeper than an excavation or a poorly organized fish study. The nation was becoming conscious of the environment, and there was Con Edison as the "villain" in a major conservation fight, slaughtering fish at its nuclear plants and threatening New York City's water supply. Even normal company operations suddenly offended refined sensibilities. The holes it dug, the smoke that poured from its plants, the transmission lines that it strung across fields and neighborhoods, the oil that spilled from its barges, even its motto "Dig We Must" seemed like deliberate annoyances. Con Edison's monopoly position, its high rates, and its political wheeling and dealing never endeared it to the public, but with the new environmental interest the company's reputation dropped to an all-time low. Adding to the problem was its poor record of service to the nation's publishing, advertising, and radio and television industries. Even Johnny Carson complained to national television audiences of the erratic billing and service of Con Edison, while *Fortune* and the *Wall Street Journal* ran major essays portraying the company as akin to a corporate leper.

In better days, when Con Edison dependably supplied energy to the nation's largest city, it might have withstood these assaults by ignoring them. But insiders, including the trustees, had to acknowledge that even by the company's traditional standards of performance it was in serious trouble. Profits were low, most of its plants were old and poorly maintained, and power failures and cutbacks had been growing in frequency since Roy Searing's death in 1957. The strains on company executives were evident in their accusations, following the 1965 court decision, that none of the summer brownouts would have been necessary if Storm King had been built. That charge may have been true on some days; but the demands on the system were so great and prolonged that it is doubtful that the short, eleven-hour spurt of energy from Storm King would have made much difference, assuming that Con Edison's base generators could have spared the power to fill the reservoir.

The worst post-Storm King incident was the November 9, 1965, blackout. Most northeastern utilities were affected, but the Con Edison system was out the longest. Company engineers were actually using flashlights and candles to reset their generators. No provision had been made for auxiliary power. Some customers had a good time that night, but most were shocked the next day as they read of surgery performed by candlelight, thousands trapped in elevators and subways, people wandering through the unlit streets of a suddenly alien city.

Wars and storms had temporarily paralyzed society before. But the blackout was no act of man or God; it was the failure of the last object of faith: machines. No one has yet been able to explain fully how it happened. A sudden surge of electrical power from Ontario, said the officials, had cascaded through transmission lines in New York State, tripping out generators in its path. It was almost a statistical impossibility, an unimaginable series of causes and effects. But if the unimaginable could happen to the northeastern power grid, what was to prevent it from occurring at a nuclear plant on the Hudson River or along the earthen dikes at Storm King?

The 1965 blackout was followed by thirty-seven other major power failures in the nation during the remainder of the decade, a disproportionate number of them affecting Con Edison. Public officials insisted on the need to build more power plants and better interconnections among utility companies. But the reaction of many citizens was a revulsion toward the technology that had let them down and shock over the environmental abuses of power production.

Con Edison's trustees responded to these complex problems with a technique that is as standard to the corporate world as is the formation of a Rockefeller study commission in times of controversy in the public sector. In 1967 Con Edison removed its top managers and brought in a new team. One of the casualties was Waring, who had devoted a career to the Storm King project and ended up being destroyed by it. The most important change was the appointment of forty-nine-year-old Charles Luce as chairman of the board. Luce's appointment seemed to pose a symbolic question: Could a decent American citizen reform an apparently indecent American corporation?

Luce's path to 4 Irving Place began in Platteville, Wisconsin, where he was born and raised. After receiving his undergraduate and law degrees from the University of Wisconsin, Luce accepted a postgraduate fellowship to Yale, where he studied under Lloyd Garrison, and later served as a clerk with Supreme Court Justice Hugo Black. Much of his adult life was spent in Walla Walla, Washington, where he raised a family, served on the legal staff of the Bonneville Power Administration, and managed one of Washington Senator Henry Jackson's election campaigns. In 1961 President Kennedy appointed Luce head of the Bonneville Power Administration. In 1966 Stewart Udall asked him to become Undersecretary of the Interior in place of John A. Carver, who was moving to the Federal Power Commission. Mr. Luce was in the department working on the Hudson River Compact Law, among other assignments, when company trustees invited him to New York.

He discovered that there were few options available to a chairman of the Consolidated Edison Company. One of his first acts was to discard the company's offensive or antiquated symbols and update its public relations program. Luce scrapped the Con Edison image of Father Knickerbocker carrying a light bulb on a silver tray, had the company's orange-colored trucks repainted blue, and changed the "Dig We Must" slogan to "Clean Energy" and then to "Conserve Energy."

Luce also took steps to reorganize the company and bring in new people. Some of the top executives, particularly the engineers, did not warm up to him. It would have been surprising if they had. He was the first chairman since George Courtelyou not to be picked from the ranks, he was a lawyer who knew little about the system, and he was a public power man.

Luce spent $750,000 to hire a management-consulting firm to examine the administrative structure of Consolidated Edison. The principal recommendation of the consultants was that the company should decentralize operations, a familiar theme. Not only was decentralization the cry in other large organizations, but the projected Consolidated Edison reorganization recalled the situation in the days of the franchised utility companies with their borough and county boundaries.

Luce discovered that it was harder for him to give away

administrative power than it had been for his predecessors to absorb it. In an age of computerized billing, intricate system planning, and expensive and complex construction projects it did not make much sense to decentralize those key decisions. About all Luce could slice off and give to the borough divisions were maintenance, motor pools, and some public relations, which meant, for example, that if a customer in Westchester County wrote a letter of complaint to Luce he would get a reply from the Con Edison vice-president for Westchester.

The new chairman did better with his personnel changes. He attracted a number of able executives and retained many who were already there. Several of the imports came from Luce's home territory in the northwest. Recruiting people to live in New York and to work for Consolidated Edison presented problems. One man, a vice-president for Southern California Edison, became Luce's chief of staff following months of negotiations. After two weeks on the job he told Luce that it would be better if he cut his obvious losses. He went back to Los Angeles.

Those who stayed were attracted mainly by Luce, to whom they were immensely loyal. Among them was Louis Roddis, Jr., a graduate of the Annapolis Naval Academy, a protégé of Admiral Hyman Rickover, a former official in the Atomic Energy Commission, and an advocate of nuclear power. Roddis became the president of Consolidated Edison. Luce's choice of a nuclear expert revealed a technical constraint on his planning to keep up with electrical demand.

The utility industry has invested little in developing alternatives to coal- and oil-burning generators, relying instead on the research programs of large manufacturers such as General

Electric and Westinghouse. The large firms have in turn deferred to the federal government, where the Atomic Energy Commission is the only agency investing research money in alternatives, and these, of course, involve nuclear fission.

In 1969 Luce published a ten-year program on how the company proposed to meet the New York area's energy requirements. His purpose was to lay out his needs so that the public and its representatives could have an opportunity to comment on them. Among the interesting revelations in the report was that 5,000 of Con Edison's proposed 6,000 megawatts of additional generating capacity were to be provided by plants located on the Hudson River. Most of them were nuclear.

The basic principle of a nuclear plant is that the heat from fission, rather than combustion, converts water into steam, and the steam drives turbines that produce electricity. Consolidated Edison's first nuclear plant—the one advocated by Searing —was opened at Indian Point in 1962. It took seven years and $142 million to build, a steep price for a 280-megawatt plant. Nuclear plants cost more than oil- or coal-fired ones, primarily because they take more time to build. Elaborate AEC technical reviews are required, and there is a scarcity of component manufacturers and a shortage of skilled labor to build and run them.

The Indian Point plant encountered other special problems that further suggest how the 1960s were disaster years for Consolidated Edison. While the plant was being built—and it was one of the first in the nation—the designers discovered that there was no turbine available that could be powered by the lower-temperature steam produced by fission compared to combustion. A supplementary oil-fired plant was installed to raise the steam temperature, but with the oil-fired plant came a conventional smokestack that emits the nitrogen oxides, sulphur dioxides, and other pollutants that nuclear plants are supposed to eliminate.

Among the theoretical advantages of nuclear plants are their comparatively low operating costs; they can be kept in operation with no complex arrangements for the import of large amounts of fuel. Instead, a truck arrives periodically carrying a small box of fissionable material. The Indian Point plant, however, encountered numerous breakdowns, the most severe being a dangerous crack in a pipe leading from the reactor; to repair the pipe Con Edison had to close down the generator for most of 1970.

When Luce arrived at the company much of the romance of nuclear power—occasioned by its novelty and by the "Atoms for Peace" program—had been replaced by technical problems such as the thermal discharge of nuclear plants, which tends to be about 30 percent greater than the heat thrown off by conventional fossil fuel plants. At the first Indian Point power station, the water that returned to the Hudson after passing through the plant was 18 degrees warmer than when it came in, which helped to account for the numerous fishkills there.

The company proceeded with construction and planning of four other nuclear plants at Indian Point and in the immediate vicinity. The concentrated heat discharge became a major problem. In addition there are the heat discharges of fifteen other power stations along the Hudson, which at the very least make it a warmer river than Henry Hudson traveled more than three centuries ago.

Roy Searing never encountered resistance to the Indian

Point complex. But Luce faced vehement opposition, mainly from people living outside Buchanan, not just over the problem of fishkills but over the more complex and potentially frightening issue of radiation. Most scientific organizations support the AEC's claim that these levels are minor, no greater than the radiation one receives in a concrete office building or on a transcontinental jet flight. But an insistent minority of scientists says that the AEC standards are too low, and that what really counts are the cumulative effects of natural radiation and the new levels being produced by man. Samples taken from the bottom of the Hudson reveal higher than normal traces of radioactivity, but since these are relatively consistent at various sample stations, it has been concluded that they are derived from the fallout of nuclear weapons testing, which has washed into the Hudson from its extensive drainage area in the northeastern United States. A clearer danger is presented by the radioactive wastes in the spent fuel. These are carted away from the Indian Point plant by trucks, transported along commercial highways, and buried in remote locations, such as abandoned salt mines in Kansas. About 75 million gallons of high-level radioactive wastes, most of them from weapons testing, are presently buried throughout the United States.

Given the real, if controlled, dangers of nuclear plants and the disagreements among scientists, public opinion is volatile and easily exploded by the sort of comment that former AEC chairman David Lilienthal made in 1961. When asked about Consolidated Edison's now discarded plan to construct a nuclear plant in Astoria, Lilienthal replied that he would not want to live in Queens if the plant were built.

The general public reaction against the Astoria plant was

mild compared with the specific legal challenges that citizen organizations mounted against the Indian Point plants. As a result of the legal groundwork established in the Storm King case, Luce found his operating license being opposed at AEC hearings by intervenors called the Citizens for the Protection of the Environment, whose members are unwilling to believe anything the company promises about safety.

In March 1970 Roddis, Luce's chief of staff, said in a speech that public distrust was perhaps the biggest problem confronting the new management at Con Edison. Roddis seemed to have in mind the recent history of the Hudson as well as of Con Edison when he said:

> *Skepticism is endemic. And with some cause. Our nation's leaders suffer from a credibility gap, as does the nation itself. Once assurances that carried the official seal were all that was needed in a more trusting time. But that day is over. People are less willing to believe what politicians tell them. . . . They don't believe scientists either, particularly government scientists. And they have some good examples to point to.*

Life is difficult for Charles Luce. He stands at the center of the contradiction in values between economic growth and natural beauty, and it is not within his power to resolve the dilemma. In a 1969 report to Con Edison customers Luce wrote: "Can the electric utilities serving 20 percent of the nation's population between Boston and Richmond continue indefinitely to double the capacity of their systems every ten or fifteen years without eventual irreparable damage to the environment? It is not too soon to begin asking such questions. . . ."

Shortly after posing this question, Luce wrote to Mayor Lindsay of New York City announcing that Con Edison would have to back off from a commitment made in 1966 that "to the fullest possible extent, power from coal- and oil-fueled plants should be generated outside city limits and brought into New York by transmission lines." The purpose of the commitment was to curb further increases in the city's air pollution levels, to which Con Edison is the largest single contributor. But now, explained Luce, a 1,600-megawatt oil-fueled plant was necessary if Con Edison was to meet projected energy demands for 1974. The plant was bitterly opposed by some members of the Lindsay administration, which subsequently authorized Con Edison to proceed with a compromise 800-megawatt plant.

THE ROAD

By the end of 1968 the Hudson River had become the most studied and protected natural resource in the United States. The enthusiastic, albeit conflicting, reaction of the public and private sectors to the popular interest in the river had produced new laws, commitments, agencies, and research.

Con Edison, in addition to supporting a fish study, had appointed a former Undersecretary of the Interior as its chairman and was pursuing the new goal of "Clean Energy." Central Hudson Gas and Electric was financing a planning program for the mid-Hudson area. The Regional Plan Association in New

York City had published a thoughtful study on needed improvements in the lower Hudson, which when added to the growing stack of Hudson River reports, including those of the Department of the Interior and the Hudson River Valley Commission, made for heavy reading. Meanwhile, New York University, the New York State Health Department, and the Federal Water Pollution Control Administration had laboratory boats on the river taking samples, checking pollution levels, and investigating how the fish survived. In Vicksburg, Mississippi, the Army Corps of Engineers built a model of the Hudson to determine, among other things, why so much silt was clogging the shipping channel to Albany. The model showed that a major cause was the canal linking the Hudson to the Harlem River, which the corps itself had blasted at Spuyten Duyvil Creek in the Bronx in 1898. The canal diverted the Hudson's flow, causing heavy silt loads to be deposited in the channel off Manhattan.

In Albany Governor Rockefeller, while waiting for the federal government to compromise on the compact agency, issued an executive order transforming the Hudson River Valley Commission into a planning organization and installed his cousin Alexander Aldrich as executive director. Aldrich set up shop in a handsome Tarrytown estate overlooking the toll plaza at the Tappan Zee Bridge. The new agency was authorized to hold public hearings on any large land development project within two miles of the river and to forward its comments to appropriate agencies. Although it lacked power, the revamped Hudson River Valley Commission performed some valuable studies, including a comprehensive mapping of the valley, a survey of historical sites, and a booklet on lighthouses. Meanwhile, New York Attorney General Louis Lefkowitz, not wishing to be outshone by the energetic antipollution prosecutions being planned by the U.S. Attorney's office in New York City, began selecting some targets for state litigation, including a Newburgh junkyard and the fishkills at Con Edison's Indian Point complex.

In Washington Secretary Udall, still firm on his conditions for a compact agency, assigned staff members to begin interim operations under Ottinger's Hudson River Compact Law, which had been passed in September 1966. The Interior Department group reviewed the environmental effects of federal or federally related projects on the Hudson and reported its findings to Udall, who was empowered to hold up any project that seemed harmful. The department stopped an Army Corps of Engineers permit to the Niagara Mohawk Power Company, which wanted to string a transmission line across the river. It also interceded in the sale of Veterans Administration property in Castleton for industrial development.

While the second round of Storm King hearings was being held at the FPC, Congress passed several laws with specific relevance to the Hudson. One was the compact bill. Another was the Transportation Act of 1966, mandating the newly formed federal Department of Transportation to assure that its projects did not adversely affect the environment and to seek alternatives to those that did. A third law, the Fish and Wildlife Coordination Act, required federal agencies to improve project coordination. Finally there was the Endangered Species Act, which gave special protection to the sturgeon of the Hudson.

The first major test of the commitments and safeguards provided by these laws was the proposed Hudson River Expressway, which had figured in the political maneuverings of Congressman Ottinger and Governor Rockefeller. Since 1965 the planned state road had grown from a local concern in Ottinger's Westchester County district to a major controversy along the river and a well-publicized issue in the metropolitan press. Scenic Hudson, the Sierra Club, and the Hudson River Fishermen's Association threw their support behind a new protest group, the Citizens Committee of the Hudson Valley, which was organized in Ottinger's district to fight the road. The Citizens Committee began by attacking the scenic impact of the expressway which would seriously affect the villages along the east bank of the river from Croton-on-Hudson to New York City. As a result of the numerous studies of the Hudson, the committee was also able to broadcast other environmental problems. The Tappan Zee area of the river, portions of which were to be filled in for the expressway project, contained shoals that were rich breeding grounds for shellfish and other aquatic life. This revelation was as startling to the public as was the news, disclosed by Robert Boyle in 1964, that most of the striped bass caught off the shores of New York and parts of New England were born in the vicinity of Storm King Mountain.

As the environmental impact of the road was debated, along with its effect on the villages and towns in the alignment, it became clear that a dramatic showdown was in the offing. Unlike the Storm King project, which was reviewed by an established agency with traditional engineering and technical priorities, the expressway would encounter new agencies and laws designed specifically to protect the environment. Moreover, the new environmentalists had gained added legal powers as a result of the Scenic Hudson decision.

Providing still more interest and complexity was the history of the road, which may be traced as far back as the 1920s, when Governor Alfred E. Smith's administration initiated large-scale road building for automobiles. The first major north-south roads in the valley were Route 9 on the east bank, for which the expressway was designed as a replacement, and Route 9W on the west bank. In the 1930s Robert Moses planned and oversaw the construction of some of the state's best highways: the Henry Hudson, Saw Mill River, and Taconic parkways on the east bank. After World War II came the Palisades Parkway on the west bank, made possible by some land contributions of John D. Rockefeller, Jr. Each road was announced as a solution to growing traffic congestion. Each road eventually fell victim to the problem it was supposed to solve.

The first major commercial expressway in the Hudson Valley corridor was the New York State Thruway, named in honor of Governor Thomas E. Dewey, whose administration built it in the 1950s. The thruway ran from the Bronx to Tarrytown on the east bank, crossed the river at the Tappan Zee Bridge to Nyack, then arched north again to Albany. Most long-distance, north-south traffic in the corridor, and virtually all truck and other commercial traffic, began using the thruway. But there was no alleviation of congestion on existing state routes and parkways. With the increase in the number of cars, buses, and trucks, there was more than enough traffic to go around. Some of the worst conditions were on the new thruway, particularly in the Tappan Zee section. On Sunday evenings in the summer, for instance, inbound New York City traffic is often backed up to the Catskills. Some state planners actually predicted the tie-up while the thruway was under construction. They urged the construction of a parallel north-south commercial expressway on the east side of the Hudson. Such a commercial expressway, they

argued, would also help reduce congestion in the east bank villages and towns north of Tarrytown, which use Route 9 as a
main street. New industries such as the General Motors plant in
Tarrytown aggravated the overcrowding, as did curb parking in
the villages, which reduced the width of Route 9. The corridor
offered a classic example of the domino effect of urbanization:
each new improvement created additional problems that in turn
required new improvements. The only real change in the picture
was a reduction in the supply of open land.

In 1957 Governor Harriman's administration announced a
new interstate highway program that seemed to encompass the
east bank expressway proposed by the state planners. The new
interstate road was to run north from the Cross Westchester Expressway about two miles in from the Hudson River to Northern Westchester. On this path the new route would also slice
through Pocantico Hills, the Rockefeller family estate in North
Tarrytown. Highway planning, never an easy assignment, is
enormously complicated when it involves the property of a future Governor.

The project was submerged from public attention until
1961—midway through Governor Rockefeller's first term—
when J. Burch McMorran, the state Superintendent of Public
Works, announced that the proposed route would be pushed
east of Pocantico Hills following a northeasterly alignment.
While there were some cynical suggestions that this new alignment was designed strictly to spare Pocantico Hills, McMorran's
reasons for the switch were persuasive. Under the original plan,
he said, the new interstate highway would dump a slug of
southbound traffic onto the already overburdened section of the
thruway between Tarrytown and the Bronx. The importance of

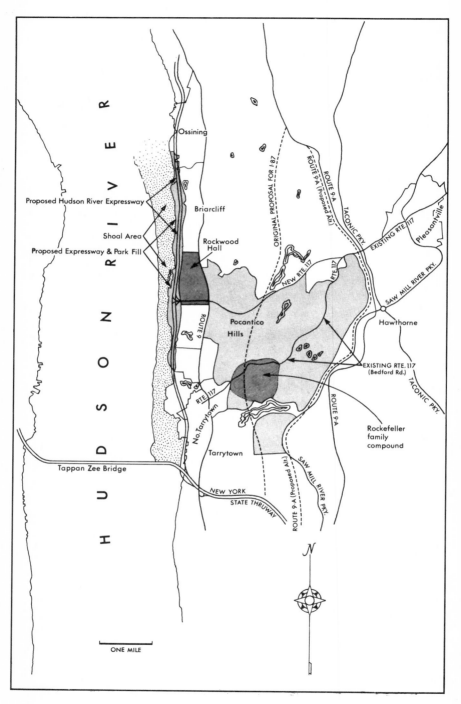

Proposed Hudson River Expressway.

McMorran's announcement was that the interstate road, as proposed by the Harriman administration, was no longer a factor in solving the corridor's traffic problems. A new east bank highway was still needed, so in 1962 McMorran and his staff began planning the disputed Hudson River Expressway.

This time the Rockefeller land obviously figured in McMorran's plans. It really had to. The 3,000-acre Pocantico Hills estate is the largest single property holding on the east bank in the vicinity of the proposed expressway. Moreover, the Rockefeller family was anxious to put its idle land to some productive use. The history of that interest goes back to 1947, when Nelson Rockefeller offered a part of the estate to the United Nations. Since then there have been some spirited family discussions over transforming a large part of Pocantico Hills into a public park or developing it for housing and commercial use. A related family concern was an existing road, Route 117, which cuts through Pocantico Hills and connects Route 9 in North Tarrytown with Route 9A to the east of the estate. Routes 9 and 9A are parallel north-south roads. The traffic and rubbernecking on Route 117 are bothersome to the Rockefellers. In 1932 John D. Rockefeller, Jr., actually offered to pay the village for half the cost of relocating Route 117 to the northern, open end of the estate, but was turned down.

McMorran had no interest in inhibiting the family's development ideas, nor did he want to worsen its Route 117 problem. Judging by the results of his early 1960s road planning, he tried to be helpful. His solution to the east bank traffic woes included the construction of the Hudson River Expressway, which would run from Croton-on-Hudson south to New York City right along the river, and the relocation of Route 117 through the undeveloped northern end of Pocantico Hills as an eastern spur of the new expressway. The new Route 117 would begin at the expressway and then cut through Rockwood Hall, the former riverside estate of William Rockefeller. After bridging Route 9, the road would pass through Pocantico Hills to Route 9A.

In 1965 the state legislature passed two bills authorizing the construction of the expressway and the new Route 117. Expressway critics later charged that the bills were pushed through the legislature under highly undemocratic procedures. The road bills, they said, lacked supporting memoranda, had not been submitted to public hearings, and had no route numbers on them. However, while the legislature's procedures were hardly commendable, they were not all that unusual. The fact is that legislative bodies are not always diligent, and the majority are often in the dark about as much as 90 percent of the laws they pass.

In July 1965, two months after Governor Rockefeller signed the road bills, McMorran met with local officials of the east bank villages to outline the solution to their local traffic problems. The expressway, he said, would require filling in portions of the river and substantial acquisition and clearance of waterfront properties. The acquisition and clearance program put many of the officials in a quandary. Solving the Route 9 congestion problem was the major political issue in some of the villages, but to most of the local leaders the loss of so much land to a non-tax-producing expressway seemed too high a price. The majority of officials opposed the expressway.

In September 1965 Governor Rockefeller compromised by announcing that the southern part of the Hudson River Expressway, the portion from Tarrytown to New York City, would be

dropped. Rockefeller's announcement reduced the official opposition, but it also cast doubts on the traffic merits of the expressway, which now had the same problem that McMorran cited
when he switched the original alignment of the interstate route:
it would dump southbound traffic from the new expressway
onto the already overburdened Tarrytown-to-New York section
of the thruway. What remained of the expressway was by normal highway standards a rather modest north-south road, ten
miles in length and six lanes in width, open to both cars and
trucks, and running from Croton-on-Hudson to the Tappan Zee
Bridge with a Route 117 spur leading eastward to Route 9A.
Approximately 3.2 million cubic yards of shoal area in the Hudson would be dredged and replaced with 9.5 million cubic yards
of fill extending 1,300 feet into the river.

The expressway plan was a major topic in the various studies of 1965–1966. In its 1966 report the Hudson River Valley Commission supported the expressway, claiming that it
would help to get the public back to the river. The report
argued that the old Hudson River Railroad right of way had
"effectively closed people off from any recreational use of the
Hudson," and that the expressway "offers a chance to reclaim
this access." The report also showed drawings of turnoffs from
the expressway to small, waterside parks.

Congressman Ottinger enlisted the aid of Secretary Udall
in disputing these claims. Udall wrote a letter to the commission, released by Ottinger, stating that "the intermingling of industrial and commercial traffic with automobile traffic does not
provide an unusual recreation resource." The Interior Department's 1966 report on the Hudson also contained some biting
comments on the expressway, including the observation that it

"would destroy public access routes to the river." The report further challenged the Hudson River Valley Commission's position by observing that "such a highway, serving commercial and industrial traffic, would seriously impair and destroy prime recreational values."

Meanwhile, the Citizens Committee of the Hudson Valley and other expressway critics charged that the waterside parks which had been included as a recreational bonus by the state in the road project and which were being praised by the Hudson River Valley Commission actually worsened the environmental impact. The Committee pointed out that the parks would require still further dredging and filling in of the Tappan Zee shoals.

Rockefeller was annoyed with these charges and the effort by Ottinger to block a state project. He was privately furious over the suggestion made by several expressway opponents that the entire purpose of the project was to benefit Pocantico Hills. He responded with some skillful political maneuvers. Through his September 1965 compromise, which had left the expressway with some technical deficiencies, he had also narrowed local opposition to one small stretch of river in Ottinger's district, where attitudes toward the project were quite diverse and opponents stood a chance of canceling each other out.

The affected villages were Tarrytown, Briarcliff, North Tarrytown, and Ossining. Tarrytown officials were adamantly opposed to the expressway. They claimed that it would upset local urban renewal plans while reducing tax revenues. Ossining officials, on the other hand, endorsed the road, which they interpreted as a solution to Ossining's severe traffic congestion. The village leaders also showed some enterprise by planning an urban renewal project in conjunction with the expressway. The new route would slice through Ossining's black ghetto, which had recently swelled with displacees from other Westchester urban renewal programs. This fact encouraged the NAACP to enter the opposition camp on behalf of the ghetto residents of Ossining. Less complex were the positions of Briarcliff and North Tarrytown, whose officials generally reflected the unwillingness of their constituents to have a truck-bearing expressway nearby.

While Ottinger and his supporters attempted to unite the diverse opposition groups under the environmental banner, the project began its trip through the elaborate new checkpoints mandated by Congress. On June 22, 1967, the Hudson River Valley Commission and the New York State Department of Public Works held joint information hearings in Ossining. The hearings were attended by about 800 people, and except for the highway officials who explained the project, all those who gave testimony were against it. Ottinger's coalition had passed its first test.

Later in the year Alexander Aldrich, the director of the Hudson River Valley Commission, reported his agency's probable position on the expressway to the Governor. In a December 1967 memorandum Aldrich revealed that his "instinct [was] that the commission will want to hold a public hearing on the expressway under our responsibility to do so whenever a project 'might impair' the scenic or other resources of the valley." He told the Governor that "it is extremely unlikely that the commission will disapprove of the road in its final findings" and promised that the "public hearing will not affect the construction schedule at all." According to one member of the commission, Aldrich wanted to skip the hearings entirely, but most of the commissioners felt that was a bit cavalier, so Aldrich was overruled. As Aldrich predicted, however, the commission later endorsed the expressway.

The position of the Hudson River Valley Commission shocked many expressway opponents, although Ottinger, at least, had never really expected a state agency to come out against the road. The true Maginot line was the federal government and the various new environmental mandates given its agencies: the Army Corps of Engineers, the Department of Transportation, and most important the Department of the Interior. The expressway required a dredge-and-fill permit from the Corps of Engineers but before the corps could issue the permit, it had to obtain the Interior Department's approval. Under the Hudson River Compact Law, Secretary Udall had been authorized to approve no project that might have "an adverse environmental impact involving any river resource having substantial natural, scenic, historic, or recreational value." Under the Endangered Species Act and the Fish and Wildlife Coordination Act Udall was also authorized to make sure that no federal activity would harm the aquatic life of the Hudson. The Department of Transportation's role concerned approval of a bridge that was to be built as part of the expressway. In its bridge review, the Department of Transportation was to assess the environmental impact of the overall project and to suggest alternatives if the impact promised to be adverse.

On January 25, 1968, Governor Rockefeller, Laurance Rockefeller, and several of their aides met with Udall in New York City, where they pressed him not to oppose the expressway. Udall was briefed on the road and told of a family decision to give part of Rockwood Hall to the state as a park. Udall was told that the park was part of the expressway package. The Secretary professed neutrality on the expressway and said that his decision would rest on his staff's review, which would begin as soon as New York formally requested the necessary dredge-and-fill permit from the Army Corps of Engineers. Meanwhile, the state started to build new Route 117 across the northern end of Pocantico Hills through to the Rockwood Hall estate. The road was beyond the purview of any environmental act and the money for it was already available. The construction of the new route before the Interior Department completed its review of the expressway unsettled the opponents. The Route 117 spur was popularly regarded as an integral part of the expressway package, and it appeared that the entire project was going ahead no matter what the Interior Department ruled. Suspicions were aroused when a Rockefeller family corporation later sold IBM a portion of the Rockwood Hall estate. The IBM site is located near the proposed intersection of Route 117 with the expressway.

On February 19 and 20, 1968, the New York State Department of Transportation, a reorganized successor to the old Department of Public Works, with McMorran as its commissioner, held formal public hearings on the expressway, which were attended by 1,500 people. Of the seventy-three witnesses who testified, only three expressed support. The day after the hearings McMorran formally applied for his Corps of Engineers dredge-and-fill permit.

Under the Hudson River Compact Law, the Interior Department had ninety days to review the request for the permit. The department's review took 270 days, during which time Ottinger tried to persuade Udall to maintain his original opposition to the expressway despite the Rockefellers' pressure. The results of the seesaw struggle became public knowledge on December 11, 1968—three weeks before Udall left office— when the Secretary authorized the Corps of Engineers to issue the permit so that construction could begin.

In a covering letter explaining his decision, Udall wrote that he had reversed his original position because of the department's findings during its review of the project. In June 1969 one Interior Department official told a congressional committee that the investigation of the expressway had been as thorough "as the average and probably more so than the average review." The records in the case have become public, so it is instructive to see what the review actually consisted of.

The political pressures placed on Secretary Udall by Ottinger and the Rockefellers are suggested by a number of documents, but none is more revealing than a memorandum written by the associate director of the Bureau of Outdoor Recreation, summarizing a telephone call he received on August 21, 1968, from Laurance Rockefeller:

> *Mr. Rockefeller said that he was with his brother, Governor Nelson Rockefeller, and he was calling to find out the status of the Interior's review under the Hudson River legislation on the application made by the State of New York to the Corps of Engineers for a permit to construct the Hudson River Expressway. . . . He wanted to be sure that Interior had not lost track of the application. . . . He added that he understood that Congressman Ottinger was putting great pressure on Secretary Udall to oppose the expressway and implied that Governor Rockefeller was prepared to exert counterpressure if necessary.*

THE ROAD

More of the political background is revealed in memoranda covering subjects not normally within the department's purview under the Fish and Wildlife Coordination Act or the Hudson River Compact Law. One department memo analyzed public reaction to the project, noting that "it is difficult to see that Governor Rockefeller would gain any political advantages. . . . By far the greatest number of people that appeared at the public hearings opposed the expressway." Another memorandum bravely explored the financial benefits of the expressway to the Rockefeller family, but ended inconclusively. The unsigned memo valued the Rockefeller park donation "at about 6 to 8 million dollars." "On the other hand," it said, "about 75 acres [of Rockefeller land] adjacent to Highways 9 and 117 would be developed commercially."

The department's inquiry into the effect of the expressway on wildlife and scenery showed far less initiative than its exploration of the political and economic impact of the road on the Rockefellers. The department's fish study consisted solely of reviewing a memorandum prepared by Kenneth Wich, a fishery biologist employed by the New York State Conservation Department. The biologist, who was given three weeks to prepare his review, was deeply concerned by the silt deposits that would be created by the dredging and filling. "It appears likely," he wrote, "that this silt load could remain in the area for a long period of time and the blockage of spawning runs could be serious." He also noted that "shellfish propagation areas represent a permanent loss." The concerns of the harried marine biologist spoke directly to the Interior Department's responsibilities under the Fish and Wildlife Coordination Act and the Endangered Species Act. Yet the department review team merely read the state-prepared memorandum and agreed that there would be some "unavoidable loss of some habitat through project construction," as one department memo put it. But the loss was dismissed as a trade-off. The "access provided the fishing and hunting public would greatly offset such losses," read the department study. This conclusion was inconsistent with the department's finding in 1966 that the expressway "would destroy public access routes to the river."

To measure the scenic effect of the expressway, the department dispatched some staff members to investigate the site of the proposed alignment. The review team was impressed with the existing Route 9, which, as its report noted, "approaches within 200 feet of the Hudson River and the Hudson River can be seen from this highway at several points." The report pointed out that "no mention has been made at any of the hearings or elsewhere that this particular section of Route 9 detracts from the scenic beauty of the Hudson." Such was the basis of the department's eventual conclusion that the expressway, which would run right along the river, presented no visual problems.

Some staff members were assigned the job of determining whether there was an alternative to the expressway. Opponents had suggested the expansion of Route 9A as a substitute. Department officials pressed the state for cost estimates of what it would take to improve 9A, which lies in fairly undeveloped terrain, to handle traffic loads comparable to those of the expressway. The state highway engineers were reluctant to make such broad estimates but eventually said that about $60 million would be required for the reconstruction of Route 9A as opposed to $139 million for the expressway. The final report by the Department of the Interior dismissed the difference, saying that "irrespective of whether or not adequate consideration has been given to prudent and feasible alternatives, it is our conclusion that this factor is not an overriding consideration in arriving at a decision of whether or not the Hudson River Expressway should be constructed."

The grounds and manner with which Secretary Udall authorized the Corps of Engineers to issue the dredge-and-fill permit for the expressway were appalling, but there was little time for opponents to contemplate the shattered network of environmental reviews. Three groups—the Sierra Club, the Village of Tarrytown, and the Citizens Committee of the Hudson Valley—moved quickly to enjoin the corps from actually giving the permit to the state. A federal district court denied the motion on February 27, 1969. The plaintiffs took the case to the Second Circuit Court of Appeals in Manhattan, which ordered the district court to hold a trial on the issues raised by the opponents. The trial began on April 16, 1969.

The legal case against the road was presented by David Sive, who was also representing the Sierra Club in the second round of FPC hearings on Storm King. Sive, a partner in a New York law firm, sandwiches environmental suits between divorces and wills. His first environmental campaign was against an attempt by Huntington Hartford to construct a café in Central Park. More recently Sive represented the Sierra Club and other organizations in their opposition to the AEC's underground nuclear explosion in the Aleutian Islands.

Sive's case against the expressway was predictable in most respects. He subpoenaed the expressway records of the state and the Department of the Interior, and as is usually the case he was given access to a room full of file cabinets with no guidance as to what was pertinent. With luck, endurance, and an office copying machine, he was able to walk away with enough memoranda to demonstrate the political pressures on Udall as well as the superficial nature of the Interior Department's expressway studies. He used the documents to argue that neither the Corps of Engineers nor the Department of the Interior had fulfilled their new environmental responsibilities mandated by Congress. He also argued that McMorran's powers to plan the expressway were too broad and that they violated due process and denied his clients equal protection under the law.

Sive's presentation took an interesting turn when he also argued that the issuance of the dredge-and-fill permit violated the 1899 Rivers and Harbors Act, a charge which had been made earlier by the Citizens Committee but seemed obscure and attracted little attention. By bringing the Rivers and Harbors Act into the case, Sive was pinning part of his clients' legal objections to the expressway to a statute that had nothing at all to do with environmental protection.

The Rivers and Harbors Act appears to have been a piece of anti-log-rolling legislation enacted by Congress in the nineteenth century to make sure that the Corps of Engineers would not perform any special local favors. The act states that "it shall not be lawful to construct or commence the construction of any bridge, dam, dike, or causeway over or in any navigable river of the United States until the consent of Congress to the building of such structures shall have been obtained."

Sive claimed that the expressway embankment was a dike and hence required congressional approval, not a dredge-and-fill permit.

The dike question reduced the expressway case to an intense level of specificity. Experts were called in, dictionaries were quoted, and expressway drawings were suppoenaed in an effort to determine whether the expressway was in fact a dike. New York State argued that the portion of the expressway facing the river was a protective embankment, a bulkhead, but not a dike, or at least not the kind of dike that controlled the flow of the river and fell within the purview of the Rivers and Harbors Act. Sive produced construction blueprints that showed the words "proposed stone dike." He also questioned government witnesses, trying to trap them into revealing the true nature of the expressway. This was his exchange with Robert Wuestefeld of the Corps of Engineers:

> SIVE: *Without the structure which is called a rock dike the river would flow further east than it would be permitted to flow. Is that correct?*
> WUESTEFELD: *That's correct.*
> SIVE: *Does it control the flow of the river?*
> WUESTEFELD: *In that connotation, it does, that's right.*

The district court judge had little patience with such interpretations. "A dike is a dike," he said in his final ruling. The corps permit violated the Rivers and Harbors Act.

The state of New York and the federal government, which had been at odds during the political maneuverings following the Storm King case, now joined forces by taking the dike ruling to the Second Circuit Court of Appeals, where they also challenged the legal standing of the Sierra Club, the Village of Tarrytown, and the Citizens Committee of the Hudson Valley. The state's brief hit the question of legal standing hard. Louis Lefkowitz's staff not only built on the FPC's original challenge of Scenic Hudson; it also leveled a strong attack against one of the expressway opponents, the Citizens Committee of the Hudson Valley, charging that the committee was nothing more than "seven self-chosen, self-perpetuating directors."

Lefkowitz's office seemed similarly outraged by the dike ruling. "By exalting form over substance," argued the state's brief, "by relying on labels rather than reality, and by failing to critically examine the function to be performed by the so-called 'dike,' the district court has seriously undermined the authority of the Corps of Engineers to issue fill permits and has delayed the start of construction on a greatly needed roadway. . . ." The federal brief dwelled on whether Congress, in light of more recent legislation, really expected the corps to seek congressional approval for dikes, even assuming that the expressway was a dike. The government argued that the dike requirement of the Rivers and Harbors Act had been superseded by later legislation, particularly the General Bridge Act of 1946 and the Transportation Act of 1966, which removed the projects listed under the 1899 statute from the need for congressional scrutiny.

The court studied these references and found that subsequent legislation had indeed exempted certain river and harbor projects, including bridges, from the requirement of congressional approval. But for some reason, not at all clear but assumed valid, Congress had said nothing about dikes since 1899. The old act was therefore still in force as it applied to dikes, and the Army had exceeded its authority by not obtaining the necessary congressional vote.

On the important issue of the opponents' right to intervene, the court did not turn away from its Scenic Hudson decision but built on it by extending legal standing to "responsible representatives of the public." The ruling was quite significant, for in 1965 the same appeals court had given impetus to citizen suits by removing the traditional economic and property requirements from a citizen's right to initiate environmental suits. Many lawyers and judges wondered whether subsequent legal developments might prompt the court to pull in the sheet. Instead, the Hudson River Expressway opinion said, in part, that

> *administrative as well as congressional concern for natural resources in the present exercise of federal authority is evident. We hold, therefore, that the public interest in environmental disputes—an interest created by statutes affecting the issuance of this permit—is a legally protected interest affording these plaintiffs, as responsible representatives of the public, standing to obtain judicial review of agency action alleged to be in contravention of that public interest.*

In June 1969 the House Subcommittee on Fisheries and Wildlife Conservation, chaired by John Dingell of Michigan, held hearings on the Hudson River Expressway. The Dingell committee had been instrumental in passing many of the new environmental laws and was anxious to determine how they were being administered. Congressman Ottinger persuaded Chairman Dingell that the expressway case might be interesting. This was to be Ottinger's last use of the hearing process to focus attention on the river and to attack Nelson Rockefeller. Ottinger relinquished his office to run for the Senate that fall.

The Dingell committee was openly contemptuous of the Department of the Interior and critical of New York State. Ottinger, together with his assistant William Kitzmiller, supplied the committee with the appropriate ammunition, most of which came from the court record. In the draft of their report, Dingell and his colleagues characterized the Interior Department's expressway review as "ex post facto efforts" to justify the Secretary's position. They also expressed "shock" and "grave concern" over the conduct of the Corps of Engineers and the Department of Transportation.

The committee seemed too busy with indignation to sense an underlying irony in the story that later came out through the work of Joseph Sax of the University of Michigan Law School. Sax was intrigued by the fact that the dike requirement of the Rivers and Harbors Act had survived so many years of supplementary legislation. He decided to investigate and concluded that it may have been nothing more than oversight. This finding suggests that while the expressway should have been stopped because of what Congress had willed, it was actually halted by virtue of what it had forgot.

The national environmental laws and policies spawned by the Hudson River disputes of the 1960s came so rapidly that there were bound to be political and administrative problems such as those pondered by the Dingell committee in the summer of 1969. There was also some judicial confusion and conflict. On the one hand the expressway decision had reaffirmed and broadened the right of citizens to sue federal agencies to enforce public environmental rights, the principle first established in the Scenic Hudson decision. Beginning in 1970 several states, led by Michigan, also enacted laws giving their citizens similar rights to sue state agencies. At the same time many judges and lawyers were clearly displeased by the development of the citizen suit as a major weapon of the environmental movement. As in the brief of the FPC in the Scenic Hudson case or the argument of the state of New York in the expressway case, the critics charged that the landmark rulings on citizen standing were too broad and that the results could be disruptive.

The clash appeared openly in September 1970 when a federal appeals court, by a two to one vote, ruled that the Sierra Club lacked legal standing to contest the development of a resort in Mineral King Valley in California. One of the specific issues in this case was the disposition of a portion of Mineral King by the Park Service to Disney Productions whose development also required the construction of a road through the Sequoia National Park. The appeals court did not allow the Sierra Club's intervention because, the court said, it lacked "private, substantive, legally protected interest" in Mineral King. That is just about the same language the FPC once used against Scenic Hudson's involvement in the Storm King deliberations.

The Sierra Club appealed to the Supreme Court. The Mineral King case was among the most important to be considered by the Nixon court, and most observers believed that it would side with the more liberal interpretation of citizen standing pioneered in the Scenic Hudson case. Surely one reason for this belief was that Chief Justice Burger was one of the first judges to build upon the Scenic Hudson decision in his United Church of Christ opinion. While the Sierra Club and its supporters were cautiously optimistic, they were also aware, largely because of recent events on the Hudson, that nothing was certain in the burgeoning field of environmental law.

On April 19, 1972, the Court ruled against the Sierra Club. Lawyers who had been involved in the Hudson River disputes feared that the gains in interpretations of citizen standing stemming from the Scenic Hudson decision had been wiped out. They were somewhat reassured after analyzing the Court's ruling, written by Justice Potter Stewart joined by Chief Justice Burger and Justices Thurgood Marshall and Byron White.

Justice Stewart wrote that the Sierra Club could not seek judicial redress on the ground that it represented the public interest in "aesthetic, conservational, and recreational" values. While reaffirming that these values are just as valid as an economic interest, Justice Stewart ruled that the Sierra Club cannot be a surrogate for the entire public nor can it claim to be injured without establishing some personal loss suffered by its members. In a dissent, Justice Blackmun interpreted the majority ruling as a simple requirement that the Sierra Club amend its complaint by providing a list of its members who actually use Mineral King and whose interest in its natural setting would be injured by the proposed Disney development. In effect, Justice Blackmun invited the Sierra Club to make the necessary change and bring its complaint back to the Supreme Court. That is probably what the Sierra Club will do.

In the meantime neither the expressway nor Scenic Hudson decisions seems affected. In both cases the litigants included organizations with a direct interest. In the expressway case the village of Tarrytown complained that the proposed road would run through the town. At Storm King several participants in the Scenic Hudson Preservation Conference were regular hikers in the Storm King area and one of the member groups maintained trails in the project site.

It is uncertain whether the Supreme Court's Mineral King ruling is a minor procedural adjustment or the beginning of more substantial curbs on citizen suits. One possible factor in future judicial rulings will be the fate of Michigan Senator Philip Hart's recently introduced bill that would have Congress give legal standing to environmental organizations. More important are the possible positions of President Nixon's most recent Court appointees, William Rehnquist and Lewis Powell, who did not take part in the Mineral King decision.

The conservative leanings of Justices Rehnquist and Powell are not helpful in predicting how they will rule on environmental cases. As environmentalism has emerged from the Hudson River Valley to become a national movement it seems clear that the politics are too new and the conflicts too deep for the responses to be predictably conservative or liberal. Instead new and unlikely alliances are being formed and a great deal of uncertainty exists as to where it will all lead.

THE BRIDGE

At sunrise on May 11, 1971, employees of the New York State Highway Department blew up the Parker E. Dunn Memorial Bridge, which spanned the Hudson between Albany and Rensselaer. The destruction of the bridge, which was only thirty-eight years old, seemed to offer a perspective on recent events on the river.

The demolition itself was managed quite efficiently. The men placed explosives along the bridge trusses and then removed themselves to a safe vantage point on the Rensselaer side of the river. Following the execution signal came puffs of smoke and a series of cracks. The span twisted abruptly, broke from the abutments, and slid diagonally into the Hudson like a torpedoed boat.

The bottom of the river is filled with objects much smaller than the Dunn Bridge. In addition to ice boxes, automobiles, and wheels, which sometimes clog the dredging machines employed by the Corps of Engineers to clear silt from the shipping channel, there are antique weapons, parts of old steamers, and remnants of railroad cars, all of which if retrieved from the lower layers of the river bottom would make the beginnings of an interesting museum.

The demolished bridge was a vivid reminder that the works of man, like men, have short lives. The rapid cycle of life and death was also suggested, less obviously, by the Cornwall waterfront, which contained the skeletons of past periods when the area was "a nest of bad company," as Nathaniel Willis described it, and then a summer colony for the rich and famous. North of Storm King, forests have reclaimed the river bank; leaves cover the foundations and the rusted barbed wire of farms that were worked early in this century.

The Dunn Bridge was opened on January 23, 1933, during a formal ceremony attended by local dignitaries and Governor and Mrs. Herbert Lehman. The reason for the excitement was that cars were still a novelty, and the bridge offered an automobile crossing between Albany and Rensselaer. Parker E. Dunn, for whom the bridge was named, was a native of Albany who had died in battle in World War I. By making the bridge a memorial to a local hero, officials and residents in the Albany area revealed the pride they took in the project, a sign of hope in a time of economic depression. The bridge created construction jobs, and the movable midspan, designed to allow ships to pass below, made the project an improvement for the shipping port in Albany.

The fanfare accompanying the dedication of the Dunn Bridge was in striking contrast to the apathy over both its destruction and its replacement, an eight-lane bridge of standard interstate design winding from Rensselaer to Albany, with Governor Rockefeller's new state office complex set in the background like the city of Oz. The new bridge was anonymous, and Parker E. Dunn's name was headed for oblivion.

The fate of the Dunn Bridge reminds us not only of the short lives of development projects, however strongly they are either applauded or opposed, but also of the changes in impact made by new projects during the course of the river's history. From the Erie Canal to the construction of river crossings such as the Dunn Bridge, America's engineers and their political supporters constructed projects offering immediate, basic improvements in people's lives. The Erie Canal, as we have seen, not only opened a wilderness and made money; it also helped to break down the manor system on the Hudson and gave rise to distinctively American institutions and attitudes.

Popular enthusiasm for vast engineering projects may be traced back to such nineteenth-century accomplishments as the Hudson River Railroad and the Storm King Highway, through to the bridge and tunnel construction earlier in this century. In his autobiography Governor Alfred E. Smith, one of the staunchest advocates of the new river crossings, offered a reminder of how basic these improvements were. Smith wrote that he became a supporter of the Hudson River tunnels during the severe winter of 1917–1918, when a shortage in New York City's coal supplies left thousands of families without heating fuel.

Some city residents died because it was impossible to get sufficient coal across the frozen river from New Jersey, where the supplies were ample.

By the time of the Storm King project man had overcome most of the river's dangers. Winter isolation, storms, and fever-bearing mosquitoes no longer plagued residents of the Hudson, though there were a few lingering annoyances such as the ferocious black flies of the upper river, which emerge in June. But urban technology had so overwhelmed the Hudson that a new set of man-made problems were created. Pollution, congestion, and scenic abuse, particularly in the New York City area, presented the possibility that the public reaction to engineering projects might change.

The impersonal and narrow purpose of the Con Edison plant helped make it the target of sudden opposition. With the exception of the tax assistance it would provide to Cornwall residents, who do not get their electricity from Con Edison, the proposed plant offered no direct benefits to the public, as did earlier engineering projects. The suggestion that the plant would produce savings for company customers was hard to believe, given Con Edison's history of continual rate hikes and insensitivity to public opinion. Claims that the project would improve Con Edison's service were also difficult to accept. This was an auxiliary plant, no more reliable than the base generators in Westchester or New York City, whose excess power would be delivered to and stored at Storm King. These base generators included nine plants built before the Depression plus newer plants such as Big Allis and Nuclear Plant 1 at Indian Point, which have been plagued by breakdowns and have contributed directly to the city's power problems.

Yet it would be wrong to interpret the opposition to Storm

King as a reaction to a uniquely incompetent company pushing an unusually insensitive plan. Con Edison has problems, but the only way they really differ from those of other large corporations may be in the degree of publicity they have received. Most corporations present their services or products to a fairly limited or dispersed clientele, and their mistakes get little widespread attention. When the lights go out in the nation's largest city and its communications center, however, the word spreads quickly.

Con Edison's project is significant for what it reveals about the changes in engineers as well as in engineering. The early engineers who reshaped the river were jacks of all trades—inventors, promoters, designers, builders, and administrators —and they worked on a wide variety of projects. John Jervis, for example, designed and built canals, dams, and aqueducts as well as railroad lines. Thomas Edison, like Jervis, worked in the shop and on the site alongside his men. Because they were individualists, economic survival forced them to develop a broad definition of who their clients were as well as a sensitivity to and pride in their work. The founder of electrical engineering actually took pains to bury his transmission lines and hide his power plants—social decencies that later electrical engineers would dismiss as too troublesome and expensive.

Motton Waring emerges from the Storm King story as the specialized bureaucrat of our time. He too was a man of varied interests, but they were neatly compartmentalized. Carpentry, gardening, and bird feeder design—avocations which his conservation opponents would doubtless approve—were strictly private occupations. At the office his exclusive function was to determine how hydroelectric pumped storage would fit into the

complex Con Edison system. The narrow technical and bureaucratic boundaries of this assignment precluded consideration of
how his project might affect scenery, fish, or even people. When
he came out of his protective cocoon to negotiate his plans, he
proved to be politically inept.

Waring was a true representative of contemporary planners, public or private, who perform their special functions behind closed doors for the approval of their corporate peers. His
plan was a pure expression of company values. The subsequent
controversy and Waring's eventual downfall were the final acts
in the thin tragedy of his innocence. He was made a villain and
then a scapegoat for merely doing what was expected of him and
what other planners are still doing. He had produced a plan
whose only virtue was that it served the needs of his employer.

The opposition to the plant also stemmed in part from narrow interest, that of the property owners in the vicinity of
Storm King Mountain. The argument presented on behalf of
gas turbines suggested that some of Scenic Hudson's supporters
were concerned only that a hydroelectric plant not be built near
them. One wonders whether they would have extended more
than sympathy to the city neighborhood that got stuck with the
gas turbines.

The public recognition that nature was important, combined with a growing revulsion at the results of bureaucratic
planning, enabled Scenic Hudson to attract support and to with-
stand a legal challenge from no less than the federal government. Cope, the clever publicist for Scenic Hudson, would be
the first to admit that his public relations campaign was fruitful
only because the nation was ready for a melodrama of this kind:
an impersonal bureaucracy stopped in its tracks before it could

claw away another scenic landscape. Garrison represented Scenic Hudson's case because of the parallels he saw between the arrogance of the New York City School Board professionals and that of the engineers of the FPC and Con Edison. Earlier Doty had taken on the fight because of the narrowness of FPC planning. The antibureaucratic theme of the Storm King and expressway struggles was also an attraction to David Sive, who recently described the environmental litigation that sprang from these two cases as "the rejection of the expertise of administrative agencies in the resolution of environmental disputes." "We believe," Sive told an audience of civil engineers, that "in any environmental controversy involving the weighing of conflicting values the weigher should be a court, a generalist rather than an administrative agency whose outlook is organically developmental and provincial."

The appeals court in the Scenic Hudson case perceived a public interest beyond the specific requirements of Orange County's work force, Con Edison's demand chart, the tax base of Cornwall, or the views and solitude of the affluent families of the Hudson Highlands. The court gave Scenic Hudson the standing to represent the public interest in the natural beauty of the area, thus paving the way for other citizen suits against the environmental impact of bureaucratic planning. But an important feature in these later disputes was the failure of the bureaucracies to respond to human needs, as the earlier canal, railroad, road, tunnel, and bridge builders had. The environmental movement sprang partly from a new appreciation of nature, but it also grew out of bureaucratic disinterest in building or planning projects that made much difference to people.

The conclusion of the expressway story offers an illustration of how environmental causes merge with and benefit from public revulsion with the bureaucracies. The federal court ruling that an expressway built on a "dike" required an act of Congress encouraged the Rockefeller administration to propose alternative routes not involving dikes. Money for the project was included in a $2.5 billion transportation bond issue submitted to voters in the fall of 1971. The bond was defeated, not because it included money for the expressway, but because of its complexity and background of bureaucratic intrigue. The bond was a hodgepodge of reimbursements for previous highway expenditures, quid pro quos among the highway and mass transit lobbies, and a circuitous subsidy to preserve a 30-cent transit fare in New York City. Only after the bond issue was turned down did the Governor declare the expressway a "dead issue."

The efforts to float a statewide transportation bond recalled the struggle in the eighteenth and nineteenth centuries over the Erie Canal project, which floundered during years of study and skepticism until DeWitt Clinton publicized its benefits to the people of New York. The transportation bond was sold even harder by a master builder and skilled politician. But Rockefeller could not break down public skepticism, resulting in part from his record, over how the state bureaucracies would actually invest all that money.

Environmentalists were less pleased with the results of the Storm King case, which suggested that there were limits to what litigation can accomplish. Following the FPC's decision to reopen its hearings so that New York City could present its objections over the proximity of the powerhouse excavation to the Moodna Tunnel, the commissioners granted Con Edison a hydroelectric license in August 1970. The commission authorized two possible sites: the Cornwall waterfront, which presented the Moodna Tunnel problem, or park land to the south side of the mountain on the site that the Palisades Park Commission had dissuaded Waring from using back in 1962. The Palisades Commission, which still wanted the powerhouse to stay out of the park, now joined with New York City, Scenic Hudson, and other conservation organizations to appeal the license.

Garrison and Butzel, on behalf of Scenic Hudson, led the attack. They charged that the FPC had ignored the court's 1965 instructions to balance natural beauty with power considerations. Generally they followed the lines of their first appeal, arguing that the commission's findings were not supported by substantial evidence and that the decision failed to comply with statutory mandates. In the first appeal the statutory argument had boiled down to Garrison's claim that natural scenery was a "beneficial public use" that Congress had given the FPC to use as a standard in reviewing license applications. But Congress had since provided a broader expression of its scenic and environmental interests through the National Environmental Policy Act, which became law on January 1, 1970, seven months before the commission licensed the plant.

NEPA, as the new act is called, had been openly criticized by many federal administrators, including FPC officials, as much too broad and therefore susceptible to bothersome citizen litigation. The act stresses, for example, the "critical importance of restoring and maintaining environmental quality to the overall welfare and development of man" and states that it is the "continuing responsibility of the federal government" to seek to improve and coordinate federal functions so as to "preserve important historic, cultural, and natural aspects of our national heritage." To fulfill this responsibility federal agencies were to "study, develop, and describe appropriate alternatives to recommended courses of action in any proposal which involves unresolved conflicts concerning alternative uses of available resources."

The Scenic Hudson brief portrayed Storm King as just the kind of resource Congress wished to protect. By challenging the FPC's evaluation of project alternatives, the evidence supporting its technical findings, and its licensing of a plant in the historic highlands, including a site in a state park, Garrison and Butzel argued that the agency had not only violated traditional legal rules and the specific mandate of the Federal Power Act but also failed to comply with NEPA. For all these reasons, said the two lawyers, the court should set aside the FPC license, not simply remand it for further hearings as was done in 1965.

The FPC countered by referring to the unprecedented length of its Storm King deliberations, the sheer size of its record, and the indisputable fact that the plant it was licensing in 1970 was somewhat different from the plant it had authorized in 1965. The powerhouse was now submerged, the Con Edison visitor center had been eliminated, the alignment of the transmission lines had been altered, and the company was now proposing to convey a portion of its site to the Palisades Park Commission. Other attempts at environmental accommodation included Con Edison's fish study and a tour of the area by the commissioners. In line with the court's 1965 instructions the FPC had also conducted a fuller study of possible alternatives such as gas turbine, nuclear, and even imported Canadian power. None could meet the technical and economic advantages of the Storm King project, said the FPC. Moreover, the commission was still accepting the claim that the hydroelectric plant might also cut down air pollution in New York City by making it possible to eliminate some older fossil fuel plants. The FPC then dealt with the basic issue of power supply. The already over-burdened Con Edison system was facing even greater strains; according to the FPC's 1970 National Power Survey, electrical demand would rise from 7,350 megawatts to 13,360 by 1980 and to 21,160 by 1990. In its license decision the FPC therefore judged that any "short-term adverse impact on the natural environment is more than offset by the enhancement of long-term productivity which will result from the project."

These arguments were presented in June 1971 to three judges of the Second Circuit Court, one of whom, Judge Hays, had written the first decision and was the only member of the court to hear both appeals. This time the court ruled in favor of the FPC by a vote of two to one. Judge Hays wrote the majority opinion, which tended to reduce the case to a technical disagreement between the FPC and Scenic Hudson over whether the commission had adequately studied alternatives to the Storm King plant. Judge Hays felt that the "environmental context" of the case did not warrant the court's intrusion into the merits of the commission's decision, and that its review should be restricted to determining whether the FPC had complied with the appropriate laws, including the court's 1965 instructions, and whether the commission's findings were supported by the evidence. He methodically reviewed the FPC's reexamination of the project and concluded that the commissioners had followed the proper procedures and standards. There was no ground on which the court could take the bold step of reversing the license decision, Hays said.

THE BRIDGE

Judge Oaks, the dissenter, was alarmed by the possibility, however slim, that the powerhouse excavation might disrupt New York City's water supply. He was also uncertain about the benefits of and the need for the plant and annoyed over the FPC's environmental review, which he felt was insufficient in view of the mandates of NEPA. His opinion for reversal will doubtless be included in any future attempt to appeal the decision to the Supreme Court. Despite state judicial reviews that have called other aspects of the project into question, prospects for such an appeal seemed slim. The outlook was made even more uncertain by the last-minute decision of Scenic Hudson's board to sign up a new law firm with Supreme Court experience to handle the appeal.

On June 19, 1972, the Supreme Court by an eight to one vote refused to hear Scenic Hudson's appeal, thus clearing what was at that time the last legal obstacle to the plant in the federal courts. Meanwhile Butzel pressed Scenic Hudson's attack in the state courts against a 1971 ruling by New York's Department of Environmental Conservation that the plant would not harm the quality of the state's waters. The seven-year war of attrition was not over yet.

The story of the Storm King battle offers an example of the adaptability of the American legal and political process and at the same time raises questions about how well the process can accommodate the growing complexity of environmental conflicts. In less than a decade a great deal has changed on the Hudson River as a result of events at Storm King. The natural environment, including natural beauty, is now a legally protected public interest. Private or public agencies representing different, sometimes opposing, interests must now face the prospect of citizen litigation. This has had some effect on the behavior of bureaucracies beyond the pronouncements of their publicity departments. The FPC offers a barometer. It is a different agency from what it was in 1965, and the practical effects of that change may be measured in the difference between the plant it licensed in 1971 and the 1965 model. A fish study has been made, the plant has been buried, there is no more visitors center. Some would dismiss the difference as cosmetic. Others familiar with what the FPC was like in 1965 would characterize the difference as significant.

The conservation movement has also changed. It is less protective and more aggressive, less conservative and more middle class. The court ruling that a person need not own property in order to express a legal interest in it may be almost as revolutionary as the removal in the nineteenth century of property ownership as a condition for voting.

Finally, the Hudson River is different, both in what has and has not happened as a result of Storm King. There is no plywood factory or pumped-storage plant at Breakneck Ridge. Instead there is a 3,500-acre state park. Now there are laboratory boats, studies, and planning agencies for the Hudson where there was once only neglect.

The clouds hanging over Storm King include the environmental crisis that has gradually emerged since the struggle broke out in 1964 and the question of whether the political and legal adjustments that have followed are really adequate. On the scale of environmental abuse, the Con Edison plant is a lightweight compared with oil spills, carcinogenic pollutants, acid rain water, and other horrors. The Storm King plant would not directly discharge radionuclides or heat into the air or water; it would merely mash some curious striped bass. The scenic problem may prove to be severe only during the construction period, when the grandeur of the mountain is reduced to the weakness of a patient undergoing major surgery. With the passage of time and the growth of the plantings, as Con Edison's attorney LeBoeuf once observed, people may regard the plant as a landmark. Unlike West Point or the Catskill Aqueduct, however, the Storm King plant may be cherished only as a reminder of the relative simplicity of the environmental controversies of the twentieth century.

Storm King was a simple dispute because it avoided causes and restricted itself to the manageable issue of whether a power plant should be built on a specific site. With the exception of some brief remarks made by Sive during the concluding oral arguments before the FPC, no one arguing the case ever questioned rising electrical demand and its crucial role in the planning of the plant or its implication for other environmentally damaging projects. Judge Oaks in his dissent was the only member of the court to introduce the forbidding demand curve into the controversy, and that was done in a footnote.

There were political and procedural reasons for this oversight, not to mention jurisdictional problems. To whom, after all, can one address the case that perhaps it is time to begin curbing electrical consumption? No agency, court, or institution deals with such a question or is in a position to do anything about it. Even within the relatively small area of the Hudson River, there is no agency or board making determinations on how much abuse the river can absorb in the interests of power production. As a result, says Merril Eisenbud, the director of New York University's School of Environmental Medicine, most of the environmental reviews of power plants or other riverside developments are merely "seat of the pants" estimates.

While environmentalists were locked in combat at Storm

POWER ALONG THE HUDSON

King, the relentless demand for electrical power encouraged Con Edison to proceed by itself or in conjunction with other utilities with plans for six other Hudson River projects: a fossil fuel plant north of Newburgh, another in Rockland County, three more nuclear plants at Indian Point, and most recently a fossil fuel plant in Ossining.

Environmental suits aimed at blocking specific projects are not only outflanked by other, perhaps equally offensive plans; they are often inconclusive, like a long, emotion-filled concert ending in a grace note. The Scenic Hudson script up to the point of the Second Circuit Court appeal is rather typical of the suits that have followed around the nation. Courts remand decisions to agencies that ask them to reconsider. The underlying assumption seems to be that the agencies can resolve the conflict if they will only try. The projects come back in amended form at best, with the agencies saying in effect: "We have thought it over, there is no other way." The projects are seldom stoppped, merely delayed.

One significant exception was provided by the California Superior Court in 1970. The setting was Los Angeles, reputed to have the nation's worst problem of air pollution. The case involved a project proposed by the Los Angeles Department of Water and Power. The court sided with the opponents by ruling against the plant, even though its absence might mean that Los Angeles citizens "may not have sufficient electrical power to supply all their peripheral needs." "But," said the court, "if the residents of the Los Angeles Basin are ever to live in an atmosphere having air of satisfactory quality, it may be essential that they be willing to make some sacrifice in the amount of electricity they use and enjoy over the next few years."

THE BRIDGE

The language of this opinion, which actually resulted in blocking the project, nonetheless conveys the guns-and-butter approach to most environmental litigation. The phrase "sacrifice in the amount of electricity they use and enjoy over the next few years" suggests that the electrical energy producers will somehow find a cleaner method of power generation, and that when they do the air conditioners may again be turned up to full speed.

Scenic Hudson's position also implied a faith in technology, a belief that if Con Edison and the FPC were pushed they would come up with a better alternative. In their first license decision the FPC commissioners succinctly stated a major theme of Scenic Hudson's case when they wrote that the opponents were arguing that "there must be another source of power as good or better." Scenic Hudson defended the mountain by preaching the virtues of gas turbines.

Yet there is no foreseeable method of power production, including gas turbines, that does not exact an environmental price, whether it be scenic disruption, air pollution, or water pollution. One of the more unsettling experiences awaiting anyone who has a deep interest in the environmental problems of power production is to listen to a Con Edison engineer discuss the implications of continuous discharges of heat into the atmosphere. One wonders why some of the engineers are not working the conservationists' side.

Scenic Hudson's restricted and optimistic view of the alternatives supports Scenic Hudson's claim to represent the unorganized public. The conflict of values that began early in the Hudson's history deepened critically in response to unchecked urban growth and bureaucratic planning that had lost contact with people by serving only institutions. While Scenic Hudson succeeded in truly representing the public's interest in the quality of its life as well as the quantity of its production and consumption, Scenic Hudson failed, as most Americans fail, to recognize the implications or deal with the causes of environmental conflict. It assumed, with characteristic American optimism, that we can have a healthy environment without giving up anything.

America's conservation fight of the century produced legal strategies and political accommodations but offered no new philosophy. It was strong on propaganda and press releases, but devoid of ideas or solutions. It offered the spectacle of the establishment fighting the establishment: corporation lawyers fighting corporation lawyers; executives at their weekend retreats battling other executives at their jobs. Ironically, it was played out in the great office towers of Manhattan.

FISHING

Would recent events on the Hudson have worked out better if
Nelson Rockefeller had maintained oyster beds in the Tappan
Zee area or fished for striped bass in the highlands? That is one
of many questions that come to mind now that I have learned
more about power production, Hudson River ecology, environmental litigation, and the kind of people who decide to oppose
pumped-storage plants. I have also learned to appreciate several
facts about the environment: that electrical appliances work as
often as they do, that the sun rose this morning, that the trees
bloomed this spring. After struggling through dispassionate

studies on pollutant levels, accumulation, and possible effects, I am also surprised to be alive and conclude that luck may be the biggest factor.

The environment should be the basic concern of our time. Suggestions of crisis are not diversions. But reducing the dangerous abuses requires a basic change in personal habits and national policies, and change does not seem likely, if only because it may be painful. Moreover, full employment, decent housing, and the elimination of poverty—goals that are just as important to the human condition as a healthy environment—presently rely on a policy of economic growth and expansion, a policy that up to now at least has accounted for much of the abuse. Readjusting the policy to account for environmental dangers involves perhaps an impossible political fight. But waiting for a recession or an environmental catastrophe to force the readjustment is too high a price. The environment therefore presents both a crisis and a dilemma.

In the absence of foreseeable dramatic solutions, one turns to second-best choices, a series of compromise approaches that together might make a significant difference. A beginning list, as far as the Hudson is concerned, would include a Governor who fished.

If the Governor had been an angler, it is doubtful that Burch McMorran would ever have proposed an expressway over the shoals of the Tappan Zee. It is also unlikely that Con Edison would have pushed a plant that endangered baby striped bass, for Governor Rockefeller gets enthusiastic over his interests and has been known to counterattack ferociously when they are threatened. It is also probable that Governor Rockefeller would have issued an executive order to his Hudson River agencies mandating fishing as a regular function for employees down to the assistant director level, which, come to think of it, might have been an excellent idea.

The question of fishing, however, is meant mainly to introduce the need for increasing the sensitivity of bureaucratic and political executives to the impact of their decisions. The narrow planning and impersonal projects that mark recent river history suggest that curriculum reforms are needed in schools of engineering, architecture, and public and business administration. The professionalism that these schools seek requires more than technical proficiency. Instruction must also cover social and environmental responsibility. The schools must shoulder some blame for the fact that while their graduates are more finely trained than earlier decision makers and builders on the river, they still have a narrow view of their social roles and seem to be less interesting as people.

Changes are also necessary on the job. While the primary purpose of a bureaucracy is economic or political survival, it does not necessarily follow that social misbehavior or environmental abuses are inevitable. Con Edison's ignorance of fish, General Motors' discharge of paint residues, and West Point's release of sanitary sewage suggest that there may be administrative solutions to some offenses. In Con Edison's case the answer might be to reassign the environmental specialist in the community relations office to an environmental section in the engineering division. If General Motors' plant manager in Tarrytown had had greater authority and money, perhaps he would have responded to the original clean-up order from the Corps of Engineers. As for the West Point example, it is clear that the federal antipollution campaign is just one of several congressional mandates that has yet to filter into the inner recesses of the Defense Department.

Means must also be found to eliminate the distance between bureaucratic decisions and their impact. Most bureaucratic decisions are similar to those of an architect who plans a building from the perspective of a wooden model he looks down on rather from the actual site where the building will be constructed. The bureaucrat's vision is worsened by the papers, maps, and verbal briefings he relies on. At Con Edison, where the view of New York City still seems represented by the "City of Light" model, the corridors of executive offices have been equipped with emergency doors, which a receptionist can close by pushing a button if a visitor seems unfriendly. Apparently insulation has become a necessary adjunct to decision making. Inside, Charles Luce and his aides try to comprehend a 600-square-mile service area containing more than 10 million people. Breaking down the doors and letting sunlight in requires a management revolution, not just a survey. Perhaps Con Edison, and society, has reached such an advanced stage of specialization and insulation that temporary job switching is called for—for example, a program under which some engineers are transferred for one- or two-year terms to the conservation organizations while lawyers like Sive and Butzel are moved into the inner recesses of Con Edison or other large corporations. The possible results are intriguing to contemplate. A step in this direction was taken in the winter of 1972, when utility executives met in a Vermont retreat with environmentalists, but the confrontation was too short.

Administrative reforms and innovations do not offer any relief to the problems of economic growth, of which power demand and supply are critical elements. Con Edison's experience over the past decade offers some important insights, including the fact that people in their homes rarely place extreme demands on the generators. The main users during peak demand periods are the office towers of Manhattan. In view of the problems that have already arisen from this fact, the demand projection for the Con Edison system—that is, a doubling every decade—can no longer be casually accepted.

Although some of the machines that contribute to the power drain perform vital social and human functions, the cutbacks of recent years have shown that there is a great deal of waste in the present pattern of consumption. If there had been no waste, the howls of protest would have been much greater during those periods when Con Edison asked some of the larger institutional users to reduce their demand while the company lowered voltage levels and even temporarily cut service to some residential areas. With the exception of a few chambers of commerce, which reacted to load shedding as though their members had been deprived of a constitutional right, most consumers behaved nicely. In fact, load shedding gave home consumers the opportunity to prove their environmental concern, and for many it improved the interior environment of office buildings designed by architects who had been oversold by lighting manufacturers.

Rather than being treated as strictly a dreadful emergency situation requiring the rapid construction of more plants, the power shortage should force a reexamination of how electricity is actually being used, the environmental price that is being paid, and whether in fact the future distribution and pricing of electricity can be helpful in achieving desirable urban policies.

Some of the implications for rates have already been perceived, such as a suggestion by Charles Luce of a rate tax to be earmarked for research on cleaner means of power production. Another possible solution is to increase charges to users during peak demand periods and reduce them during off-peak hours. A tax incentive to encourage appliance manufacturers to design equipment requiring less electricity is still another of many possibilities.

As long as the rising demand curve is accepted as a goal to be achieved, we may also miss seeing the possibility of using shortages to attain desirable goals. For example, one way of alleviating Con Edison's problems is to level off its peak demand. The company has more electrical-generating capacity than it knows what to do with at night and in the early morning. In other words, like New York City's telephone service, its streets, and its rapid transit, Con Edison faces a nine-to-five problem that, like the others, could be overcome with staggered work hours. As an effective tool of urban planning, the power crisis could even be put to daring use to curb more growth and congestion, as London has tried, but with legal procedures. By imposing limits on available power, New York City could begin to check the growth that has overwhelmed its institutions and weakened their ability to provide basic services either efficiently or democratically. This obviously is not a firm recommendation, but merely an indication of the kind of idea the power problem should be generating but is not because the utilities and their regulators are programed to raise their demand projections rather than to reexamine them. Among the maddening results of their conduct is the further deterioration of the Hudson.

Apart from the changes that must be made within the institutions that use the river, the Hudson obviously needs money.

Some of the best recommendations on how funds could be invested were contained in the 1966 report of the Hudson River Valley Commission. The report might have devoted more attention to the river mayors, who should be paid more and serve full time so that their jobs will be more attractive. The villages and towns of the Hudson are in a difficult transition from a worn-out nineteenth-century economy to a new, as yet unclear, twentieth-century role. One central fact should dictate their future. The best-planned and most sought after residential communities in America are built around lakes, often artificial. The villages and towns of the Hudson look out on one of the great rivers in the world. Lack of new construction is a short-term problem. The key issue is how to control the development that is bound to come while preserving the good architecture that is already there. The river could use one or two demonstrations of how that goal can be achieved.

Property tax reform is probably the single most effective device for saving the Hudson's remaining beauty and for preventing the river from becoming a cooling trough for power plants. Beginning with the 1971 *Serrano* v. *Priest* decision in California, disparities in local property wealth have already been singled out by both state and federal courts as contributing to unequal educational opportunities. The judicial finding that a child's wealth should not be a function of his parents' or neighbors' wealth might well be applied to an environmental resource such as Storm King Mountain, which had the misfortune of being located in the economically depressed village of Cornwall. It could even be applied to the entire Hudson River, which happens to flow by many impoverished towns and cities.

The direct relationship between meager local property

wealth and environmental abuse was amply demonstrated in Cornwall and Buchanan, where low assessments and tax rates meant, in effect, cheap sites and docile local officials for Con Edison's planners. Mayors Donohue and Burke can hardly be faulted for welcoming a major tax producer, but the tax system that encouraged their behavior needs overhaul. One clear solution is increased state aid based on larger state income taxes and a statewide property tax levied on uniform assessments and rates, plus an equalization formula for distribution that takes away the economic handicap of the Hudson River localities. As long as the local property tax remains the principal means of financing local budgets, river mayors will continue to sell off the scenery.

The river can be made fit for swimming. That is the standard set by the current clean-up campaign, and with enough money the goal can be achieved, according to every sanitary engineer and marine biologist I have talked to.

Among the good trends on the river is growing student interest. The young can be expected to pay still greater attention to the Hudson if only because they will have to. According to the Army Corps of Engineers the Hudson will become a major new source of fresh water for areas of the northeast whose supplies are desperately short. The use of a polluted river for drinking water is not new. People in the Delaware Valley, for example, have been contaminating their water supply for many years and have grown accustomed to it. The Hudson, however, is used sparingly at the present. Tapping it for domestic consumption will provide a new experience and may greatly enhance the river's image. It will also produce bitter controversy. Poughkeepsie, for instance, already taps the river at a point perilously close to the existing salt water line.

FISHING

Another coming attraction on the river will be its abundance of open space. Despite the popular conception that the Hudson is an urban river, only 8 percent of its drainage area is urbanized. The rest is forest and farmland. The existence of this bounty, as we have seen, may be traced to the early patroon and manor systems. Up to now the restriction of land ownership to families of means has had a restraining influence on development compared to other areas where land was distributed more democratically. But the old estates are now breaking up, making the preservation of scenic land an urgent priority. Right now the Hudson Valley, from the highlands north, is the largest and scenically richest area of open space in the New York metropolitan area.

Student interest in the Hudson offers some chance for unusual education programs, particularly in the high school grades. An entire semester could be devoted to the river's ecology, geology, and history. These topics could be buttressed with courses on the architecture, literature, and art of the river. Trips, hikes, and camping could make the curriculum come alive. The Hudson is not only a beautiful river; it is an environmental laboratory and presents a complete picture of American civilization.

The Hudson, despite some of the unique features of its history, has always revealed a great deal about the people who live along it as well as about national trends and values. Right now the river presents a confusing scene, a jumble of symbols representing beauty and ugliness, charity and greed, hope and despair. Many of the physical symbols suggest both individual and institutional indecencies such as a rotting auto hulk sitting in a tidal marsh and a discharge pipe pouring forth an ugly liquid. What the Hudson and the nation need immediately are acts, not words, proving that the institutions care and providing stimuli to which individuals can respond. The cumulative effect will improve both behavior and appearance.

How the Hudson will look in ten or twenty years is very important but impossible to predict. Whatever its appearance, it will undoubtedly still say a lot about us and our nation. The Hudson of the future, like the Hudson of the present, will be exactly what we deserve.

ACKNOWLEDGMENTS
AND BIBLIOGRAPHY

The research on this book was undertaken with the help of a travel and study award from the Ford Foundation. I am grateful for the Foundation's support and appreciate the personal encouragement of Gordon Harrison, Louis Winnick, Mitchell Sviridoff, and Robert Goldmann.

My sources range from authors who wrote of the river's past to technicians who told me about their present work. I am indebted to all of them. In the following narrative, I describe my sources for each chapter except the first, which is a summary introduction to the book, and the last, which is my tentative interpretation of the lessons implied in the recent history of the Hudson.

THE MOUNTAIN

With the exception of Robert Juet's log of the voyage of the *Half Moon,* all of my historical material is based on secondary sources. Carl Carmer's *The Hudson* (New York 1939) was my starting point. In an interview Carmer warned me that his book was "the work of a poet, not an historian," yet for its combination of folklore, fact, and good reading, it still may have no equal among the hundreds of books that have been written on the general history of the Hudson. Besides introducing me to what I should read and see, Carmer was also an eyewitness to the early days of Scenic Hudson. Another walking encyclopedia of Hudson River history was Benjamin Frazier of Garrison, whose interests dwell mainly on the Hudson Highlands. Like Carmer, Frazier also was involved in the origins of Scenic Hudson.

Benson J. Lossing's *The Hudson from the Wilderness to the Sea* (New York 1866) and the first two volumes of Nelson Greene's *History of the Valley of the Hudson: River of Destiny* (Chicago 1933) were filled with useful information. I also learned from and enjoyed reading *Hudson River Landings* (Indianapolis 1933) by Paul Wilstach.

Christopher J. Schuberth's *The Geology of New York City and Environs* (Garden City 1968) told me all I felt I needed to know about the geological history of the Hudson Highlands, particularly after I had read the F.P.C. testimony on Project 2338 of C. P. Benzinger, a geologist of Uhl, Hall, and Rich (Vol. 80) and the contradictory testimony of A. Scott Warthin, Jr. (Vols. 33 & 85), a geologist at Vassar College. The Storm King Highway is featured prominently in Bruce Wallace's *Hudson River Guide and Map,* which was produced sometime in the 1880's for vacationers. The highway is mentioned in many Hudson River books, but I was unable to uncover details about how it was built.

For mid nineteenth-century life in Cornwall I relied heavily on *Out of Doors at Idlewild* (New York 1855) by Nathaniel Parker Willis. Idlewild was Willis' Cornwall home to which he retreated in 1850 after a migratory literary career. In this book Willis began his campaign to rename Butter Hill. A reprint of Willis' *American Scenery* (Barre, Mass., Imprint Society 1971), with W. H. Barlett engravings, was also invaluable for getting a flavor of nineteenth-century life on the river.

My suggestion that Butter Hill may be a mispronunciation of Buttel Hill is based on a heavily marked up copy of *Visit to the Falls of Niagara* (London 1826) by John Maude, in which an unidentified editor writes that early river maps designate the mountain as Buttel Hill. Sure enough, the anonymous editor is correct. A more accepted version of how Butter Hill got its name is that the U.S. Navy procured its butter supplies from the farms in the Orange County, Storm King area.

For the early settlement of the Hudson Valley I learned a great deal from *A Short History of New York State* (Ithaca 1957) by David M. Ellis, James A. Frost, Harold C. Syrett, and Harry J. Carman. These authors introduced me to many areas of state history I knew nothing about and helped me to relate river developments to broader regional and national events. Their book has recently been revised with an excellent bibliography. It is an unusually informative, well written, and comprehensive history of New York.

For supplementary reading on the colonial period I used *A*

ACKNOWLEDGMENTS AND BIBLIOGRAPHY

Maritime History of New York (Garden City 1941) which was a production of the Writer's Program of the Works Progress Administration. Extremely helpful were the pictures and maps in I. N. P. Stokes' *The Iconography of Manhattan Island, 1498–1909* (New York 1967). It was interesting to read James Morris' comments on all periods of river history in *The Great Port: A Passage Through New York* (New York 1969), a gracefully written book with an unlikely sponsor, the Port of New York Authority.

The little that I know about Indians came from E. M. Ruttenber's *History of the Indian Tribes of Hudson's River* (Albany 1872). The problems between the tenants and manor lords were presented in *Agrarian Conflicts in Colonial New York 1711–1775* (New York 1940) by Irving Mark. A pleasant view of life on the manors is provided in *Philipsburg Manor,* published in 1969 by Sleepy Hollow Restoration. A glimpse of how the manor grant evolved into the present is offered in Charles W. Snells' *Vanderbilt Mansion,* prepared in 1960 for the National Park Service.

THE CANAL

For the political background to the Erie Canal story I relied on Dixon Ryan Fox's "Decline of Aristocracy in the Politics of New York State," *Columbia University Studies in History, Economics and Public Law* LXXXVI, 1919. Also pertinent was *Politics in New York State 1800–1830* (Syracuse 1965) by Alvin Kass. There are many good books on the Erie Canal, but the ones I found most useful were: *Low Bridge! Folklore and the Erie Canal* (Syracuse 1962) by Lionel D. Wylel; *Bridges, Canals, and Tunnels* written by David Jacobs and Anthony Neville and published by American Heritage and the Smithsonian Institution in 1968; and *Canals and American Economic Development* (New York 1961) edited by Carter Goodrich. Goodrich's book is most instructive, particularly Julius Rubin's essay on the Erie Canal from which I lifted the Jefferson and Franklin quotations. An unexpected windfall of Erie Canal information was *The Erie Canal: Gateway to Empire* (New York 1963) by Barbara and Warren Walker. The Walkers' book was a demonstration of how to prepare a research paper. By assembling such documents as Clinton's report, engineering surveys, and local reaction to the project as a model of the kinds of sources a paper should rely on, the Walkers saved me a lot of work and I am grateful. I did not come across a biography worthy of Clinton, particularly in view of my interpretation of Clinton as a political prototype.

Anthony Bailey's piece on the Hudson River in the July 29, 1967, *New Yorker* contained Captain Marryat's thoughts on the river. The sources for the other traveler's observations on the changes along the river were: *Travels Through the States of North America, and the Provinces of Upper and Lower Canada, During the Years 1795, 1796, and 1797* (London 1807) by Isaac Weld, Jr.; *Travels Through Canada and the United States of North America in the years 1806, 1807* (London 1816) by John Lambert; and *Letters About the Hudson River and Its Vicinity* (1837) by Freeman Hunt.

Among the many books written on the steamships of the Hudson, I used Donald Ringwald's *Hudson River Dayline: The Story of a Great Steamship Company* (Berkeley 1965) and *Old Steamboat Days on the Hudson River* (New York 1907) by David L. Buckman. Buckman's father was the captain of the *North America,* one of the river's famous nineteenth-century steamers.

ACKNOWLEDGMENTS AND BIBLIOGRAPHY

For the story of the railroads of the Hudson and Mohawk valleys I turned to *Men and Iron: The History of the Central* (New York 1938) by Thomas Y. Cromwell. Less puffy and more detailed was F. W. Stevens' *The Beginnings of the New York Central* (New York 1926). Alvin Harlow's *Road of the Century* (New York 1948) seemed the best of the lot. Each of these books incorporated some of the Hudson River Railroad story, but for supplementary information I used John B. Jervis' *Report on the Hudson River Railroad* (Poughkeepsie 1846) and *The Hudson River Railroad Route* (New York 1874) by Charles Taintor.

Two books helped me to appreciate the early, silent conflicts between the values of the artists and the engineers. The first was *The Catskill Mountain House* (New Brunswick 1966), Roland Van Zandt's allegorical treatment of the rise and decline of one of America's most famous resorts. The second was Leo Marx's *The Machine in the Garden: Technology and the Pastoral Ideal in America* (New York 1964). I looked up the Marx book after reading his "American Institutions and Ecological Idealism" in the November, 1970, issue of *Science,* in which Marx argued that ecology springs from American writing and that the ecological movement may represent a convergence of American literary and scientific thought. Van Zandt's book directed me to some of the works of Bryant, Irving, and Cooper which seem especially relevant in this time of environmental crisis. Those interested in probing the relevance further should read Donald R. Noble's "James Fenimore Cooper and the Environment," which was the lead article in the October, 1971, issue of *The Conservationist,* a bimonthly magazine published by the New York State Department of Environmental Conservation. The conflict between America's pastoral and urban impulses is also treated in Henry Nash Smith's *The American West as Symbol and*

Myth (Boston 1950), from which I gained much more on a second reading than I did when I was a student. Frederick A. Sweet's *The Hudson River School and the Early American Landscape Tradition* (New York 1945) and *Three Hundred Years of American Painting* (New York 1957) by Alexander Eliot were my sources for the work of the Hudson River School.

THE COMPANY

For the early history of Con Edison I went to the company library where there was an ample supply of pamphlets, reports, and newspaper clips. The most useful single source was the *Consolidated Gas Company of New York, A History Published by the Company in the Fiftieth Year of Its Existence as a Corporation and the One Hundred and Tenth Year of Continuous Service to the People of the City of New York* (New York 1934). This authorized history, prepared by Frederick L. Collins, sets out in refreshing innocence how the gas companies got started, including, for example, how the members of the various official city study commissions of the gas business were often directors of the gas companies.

For that part of Con Edison's story tied to the exploits of the Robber Barons I used Matthew Josephson's *The Robber Barons* (New York 1934) and *The Politicos* (New York 1938). I also found W. J. Lane's *Commodore Vanderbilt* (New York 1942) to be helpful. *The Great Pierpont Morgan* (New York 1949) by Frederick Lewis Allen was my general primer on Morgan, which I supplemented with the personal insights provided by Herbert L. Satterlee's descriptions of his father-in-law's interests in electricity, the West Shore Line, and life at Cragston in the biography *J. Pierpont Morgan: An Intimate Portrait* (New York 1939).

ACKNOWLEDGMENTS AND BIBLIOGRAPHY

A description of how the financiers backed Thomas Edison's work and eventually brought the Edison companies of New York City under the banner of Consolidated Gas is contained in Payson Jones' "Consolidated Edison System Power History," an apparently unpublished manuscript completed in 1940 and available in mimeographed form in the Con Edison library. Another authorized company history entitled *Forty Years of Edison Service 1882–1922* (New York 1922) by T. Commerford Martin was also helpful. Throughout this chapter I relied for background material on J. W. Hammond's *Men and Volts* (New York 1941).

POWER

The private preoccupation of the robber barons with matters of beauty is portrayed in their biographies and nicely tied together in portions of Stephen Birmingham's *The Right People* (New York 1958). A contemporary view of their feuds, noblesse oblige, and personal characteristics is also contained in *Recollections of an Old New Yorker* (New York 1932) by Frederick Van Wyck. The impact of the barons on the cultural life of the city is skillfully captured in *Merchants and Masterpieces: The Story of the Metropolitan Museum of Art* (London 1970) by Calvin Tompkins.

When I began this book, I knew nothing of the history of the conservation movement in America or along the Hudson. Local background is offered in *Fifty Years of Conservation in New York State 1885–1935* by Garth A. Whipple (Albany 1935). For the national picture I relied principally on *The American Environment: Readings in the History of Conservation* (Reading, Mass. 1968) edited by Roderick Nash and *Perspectives On Conservation: Essays on America's Natural Resources* (Baltimore 1958) edited by Henry Jarrett.

ACKNOWLEDGMENTS AND BIBLIOGRAPHY

The impact of the barons on city planning, particularly the city beautiful movement, is suggested in parts of James Marston Fitch's *American Building: The Historical Forces Which Shaped It* (Cambridge 1966). The Fitch book also discusses the role of electricity and business practices on the shape of buildings and cities, as does Carl W. Condit's *American Building* (Chicago 1968).

My source for the story of James Stillman's plans for Storm King Mountain was Stillman's grandson, Calvin Stillman, who has a home in Cornwall and is known locally as one of the "mountain people." Stillman also gave me considerable information on the local reaction to the plant which he has written about in "The Issues in the Storm King Controversy," *Black Rock Forest Papers*, No. 27 (Cornwall 1966). The investigations of the company in 1904 are covered in the first volume of M. L. Pusey's *Charles Evans Hughes* (New York 1951) from the point of view of the crusader. I found no comprehensive account of Con Edison's growth between the two world wars. Robert Moses met with me to discuss his recollections beyond those contained in his *Public Works: A Dangerous Trade* (New York 1970), which has interesting material on the utilities plus abundant evidence of Moses' great affection for Governor Alfred E. Smith. My other sources for Governor Smith were *Al Smith: Hero of the Cities, a Political Portrait Drawing on the Papers of Frances Perkins* (Boston 1969) by Matthew and Hanna Josephson; and *Up to Now: An Autobiography* (New York 1929) by Alfred E. Smith. *Franklin D. Roosevelt as Governor of New York State* (New York 1955) by Bernard Bellush was my source for FDR's struggles with the utilities. Fiorello LaGuardia's biographers do not dwell on the mayor's battles with Con Edison although the encounters are covered in "Consolidated Edison Company of New York," a 1968 case study produced by the Harvard Business School, which helped me in understanding other aspects of Con Edison's

more recent history. Another report, "Chronology of Important Events 1930–1962," which was prepared by Con Edison's public relations staff in 1962, aided me in piecing together recent company developments.

Richard R. Lingeman's *Don't You Know There's a War On? The American Home Front 1941–45* (New York 1970) suggested the long range problems created by the maintenance and construction hiatus of World War II. Thomas E. Duncan, Jr., the recently-retired Executive Vice President of Con Edison, spelled out the implications for Con Edison and the utility industry. The background of Con Edison's race against crisis was also outlined to me by J. T. Kirdahy, Jr., an engineer in the company's System Planning Department who gave me a general briefing on how the system works. Tours of Con Edison plants, new and old, were arranged by Jerry Halvorsen, Coordinator for Environmental Affairs, who also steered me to the necessary technical literature. Edward Burkhart, a 40 year company veteran, took me through the company control center, explained how it worked, and reflected on the changes he had seen during his tenure. My view of life at the plant level was supplemented by some former schoolmates from Bayside High School and P.S. 94 in Queens who now work at Con Edison.

The importance of Hudson Searing's reign was brought to my attention by Robert Moses. Searing and the present company chairman, Charles Luce, are among the few utility executives that Moses regards as competent. Searing's importance was verified by some of the older company executives and employees I spoke with.

THE PLAN

The complete record on Project 2338 is rather extensive. The Federal Power Commission in Washington has all of it for public examination. For the details on the plan and its various amendments I used the reports of the hearing examiner and the direct testimony of consultants from Uhl, Hall, and Rich and company executives, particularly M. L. Waring. Waring was extremely kind and generous in his willingness to sit down and tell me how he went about planning the plant. Much of my narrative at the opening of Chapter VI is based on our conversation.

Marion Mailler, who recently stepped down as the publisher of the *Cornwall Local,* was a major source for information on the local impact of the plant. Mrs. Mailler indicated whom I should see, helped arrange interviews, and introduced me to some of the older village residents who told me their recollections of Cornwall's past as a major resort area. I particularly enjoyed Charles Slater's willingness to accompany me to the site of the powerhouse, i.e. the village water front, to tell me and show me in photographs what it was once like, and to take me to the site of his childhood home, which he recently sold to Con Edison. A cogent summary of Cornwall's history is provided in "Cornwall: A Glimpse into its Past," a paper prepared by Alice B. Hume, Cornwall's official historian. Mayor Donohue gave me a pleasant official welcome to Cornwall on his veranda where we talked of the local conflict, his original reaction to the plant, and his lingering hopes for improving Cornwall with the plant taxes. Mayor Burke of Buchanan gave me an equally cordial welcome and tour of Buchanan. The DeSapio-Marcus intrigues concerning the Aqueduct are well covered in *The New York Times* and have become the subject of a recently-published and fascinating book, *A Percentage of the Take* (New York 1971) by Walter Goodman.

William Osborn, former President of the Hudson River Conservation Society, added to the knowledge I gained from Waring about the transmission line negotiations. Osborn also told me his side to the story of the controversy within the Society. Helmut Kempel was the reporter from *The Middletown Record* who uncovered the payment arrangement between Con Edison and the village attorney. The story appeared in the April 16, 1968, issue of the paper. Waring, Donohue, and George Delaney, Con Edison's director of Community Relations, gave me the village and company version.

CONFLICT

Rod Vandivert, the executive director, and Terry Rotola, the executive secretary of Scenic Hudson, work in the midst of cartons and file cabinets of information on the Storm King case in a small section of the 16th floor of 500 Fifth Avenue. Vandivert, who became the executive director in the spring of 1965, does not figure in my narrative, which deals mainly with legal developments. His role as a spokesman and political trouble shooter has been crucial for Scenic Hudson and his help to me was considerable. Mrs. Rotola's help goes far beyond knowing what is in the cartons and boxes, for she has been with Scenic Hudson from the start and probably knows more than anyone about the story of the organization. In addition to Vandivert's and Mrs. Rotola's help, I could have never pieced together Scenic Hudson's evolution without access to its files, particularly the complete record of newspaper clips on the controversy. Many reporters have covered the Storm King beat, and while I have benefited from all of them, I would like to single out the lucid reporting of McCandlish Phillips and David Bird in *The New York Times* and William G. Wing's excellent four part series on the controversy, which appeared in the May 3–6, 1964, *New York Herald Tribune*. I also went on several Scenic Hudson outings during which I had a chance to meet some of its supporters. Because Scenic Hudson is a somewhat unstructured organization, it was hard to determine whom among its supporters I should talk to extensively. My main sources during extended interviews were Stephen Duggan, Benjamin Frazier, Alexander Saunders, Walter Boardman, Robert Boyle, Carl Carmer, and, for briefer discussions, Susan Reed. Nancy Mathews, who as an employee of the Sierra Club and now an assistant to David Sive has played a major role in most of the recent environmental struggles on the river, gave me extremely helpful insights and suggestions on whom I should talk to on all sides of the conflicts covered in the book.

Dale C. Doty told me of his role in the case. He also gave me access to some of his files and a rundown on the background and personalities at the Federal Power Commission. James Cope and William Kitzmiller discussed their contributions, although my assessment of their major roles is based on what others said. Robert Boyle and his book, *The Hudson River: A Natural and Unnatural History* (New York 1969), were extremely helpful not only in understanding the fish issue at Storm King and the origins of the Hudson River Fishermen's Association, but in introducing me to the natural history of the Hudson. I learned much from Mr. Boyle. His book also has an excellent bibliography. Con Edison's side of the fish question was presented in the FPC testimony (Vols. 39 and 32B) of Alfred Perlmutter of New York University. I also gained information from a report, "Ecology of Anadromous Fish of the Hudson River" prepared for the House Subcommitee on Fisheries and Wildlife Conservation in 1969 by John Clark of the US Bureau of Sport Fisheries and Wildlife, Sandy Hook Marine Laboratory in Highlands, New Jersey. The Hudson River Spawning Grounds were the subject of hearings on May 10 and 11, 1965, by the Subcommittee on Fisheries and Wildlife Conservation, i.e., the Thompson Sub-committee.

My narrative on the FPC hearings of early 1964 is based on the hearing transcript. The point about the difficulty of citizen groups in obtaining technical consultants is based on my experience, but it was also underlined in hearings held by the Committee on Commerce of the United States Senate during May 4–6, 1966, on the subject of overhead and underground transmission lines. For the question of the regulations governing the location and siting of power plants I relied on "Laws and Procedures Of Power Plant Siting in New England" a 1970 report by the New England River Basins Commission. Some good background to this issue was also presented in "Land Use: Congress Taking Up Conflict over Power Plants" an article which appeared in the November 13, 1970, issue of *Science*.

THE TRIAL

Frances Francis, formerly special counsel to Commissioner Ross, gave me an objective and sympathetic view of the problems and priorities of the FPC, and was also helpful in suggesting whom among the civil service employees I should talk to. Mrs. Francis, former General Counsel Richard Solomon, and Commissioner Ross were my principal sources for the behind-the-scenes attitude of the Commission toward the Storm King case. I did not interview all the commissioners, but relied instead on their recorded comments from the transcript of the first oral arguments and my observations during the second, and final, oral arguments on the case.

I also witnessed some of the hearing room performances of the lawyers. In addition, I interviewed Lloyd Garrison and also Albert

ACKNOWLEDGMENTS AND BIBLIOGRAPHY

Butzel, who spent many hours with me trying to improve my understanding of the legal issues. Jane Lee Eddy and John Simon of the Taconic Foundation talked to me about Stephen Currier's interest in the case. The written sources were the court decision, transcript, and the briefs from the FPC, Scenic Hudson, and Con Edison. For the Con Edison side I talked with Carl Hobelman of LeBoeuf, Lamb, Lieby and MacRae. Because of the importance of the case, I would like to mention those lawyers whose names do not appear in my narrative but who made substantial contributions to my knowledge. Frank Potter and Alan Feld helped Garrison in the second round of FPC hearings. Cameron MacRae eventually took over for LeBoeuf in arguing on behalf of Con Edison and, in addition to Hobelman, was assisted by Peter Bergen, Sheila Marshall, Jeffrey Silver, and Albert Froh.

Charles Reich's "The Law of the Planned Society," which appeared in the July, 1966, *Yale Law Journal* helped me to understand some of the impact of the Scenic Hudson decision on administrative law as did Seder's "Regulatory Activism—the Aftermath of Scenic Hudson," which appeared in the 1969 Annual Report of the American Bar Association. Joseph L. Sax's *Defending the Environment: A Strategy for Citizen Action* (New York 1971) traced some of the impact of the Scenic Hudson decision while arguing the need to keep the bureaucracies honest via citizen suits. Sax also produced an account of the FPC proceedings on the Storm King case in *Water Law, Planning and Policy* (Indianapolis 1968), which I found helpful and which is a good source for those who want to know more than I have given about the second round of FPC hearings. My reason for treading lightly on the second round is that the issues raised by the 1965 court decision merged afterward with other river disputes, and what interested me most was how all river agencies, not just the FPC, would respond to the new interest in the river and the environment.

POLITICS

In this chapter I began to draw on my experiences and observations with the New York State Urban Development Corporation. For my comments on the Governor I was also able to use the many books that have been written about the Rockefeller family, none of which seemed more informative than Raymond Fosdick's sympathetic, insider's account, *John D. Rockefeller, Jr.: A Portrait* (New York 1957). The similarities between the Governor's varied and sometimes contradictory philanthropic, conservation, and building interests and those attributed to his father by Mr. Fosdick became quite apparent after reading *Our Environment Can Be Saved* (Garden City 1970) by Nelson A. Rockefeller.

The ubiquitous Mr. Kitzmiller spent two days going over Congressman Ottinger's wars with the Governor. I was permitted to see some of the fiery correspondence between Ottinger and the Rockefellers in which the combatants adhered to proper decorum by addressing each other by their first names or concluding with "Best regards, Nelson."

For background on the Hudson River Valley Commission I went to Bruce Howlett, the former Deputy Director and Carl Mays, a commissioner who succeeded Aldrich in 1969 as the executive director. Mr. Mays was previously the Planning Director for Orange County and was helpful also in giving me his insights on the Storm King case.

My material on the Ottinger bill to make the Hudson a national scenic riverway and the reactions to the idea are taken from hearings on the bill before the House Subcommittee on National Parks and Recreation. In these hearings, held on July 24 and 25, 1965, one can also see the dawning of the Hudson River Expressway controversy. My summaries of the various study reports are taken from: *The Hudson: The Report of the Hudson River Valley Commission 1966;* and *Focus on the Hudson: Evaluation of Proposals and Alternatives* produced by the Department of Interior in 1966. Agency responsibilities for the Hudson River were compiled in *Existing Approaches to Water Resources Administration: Interstate, Federal, State, Intrastate, and Local Water Resources Agencies by Function,* a staff report by Stuart Graham and John Harder prepared in 1968 for the Hudson Valley Commission.

The literature on pollution is endless. For his continuing help in wading through it and answering my questions I am most grateful to Max Boudakian, a friend and research chemist. For a list of who is dumping what I relied on the testimony and appendix of a presentation made on June 18, 1968, to the Federal Enforcement Conference on Pollution of the Hudson River and the Interstate Tributaries between New York and New Jersey by Paul Eastman, Assistant Commissioner, Division of Pure Waters of the New York State Department of Health. My source for the scope of the refuse acts and the Corps of Engineers' responsibilities was an article entitled "Adding New Bite to an Old Pollution Control Law," which appeared in the January 6, 1971, issue of *Chemical Week.* Criticism of the Nixon administration's use of the refuse acts was contained in "Water Pollution: Conservationists Criticize New Permit Program" in the January 22, 1971, issue of *Science.* For the federal approach to refuse act indictments along the Hudson I talked with John Burns III, and his former boss Whitney North Seymour, Jr.

The 1968 Harvard Business School case study on Con Edison

provided a convenient source of factual evidence on the conditions Charles Luce encountered when he took over the company in August, 1967. The *Fortune* article I referred to was entitled "Con Edison: The Company You Love to Hate," and appeared in the March, 1966, issue. The *Wall Street Journal* account of Con Edison entitled "The Unhappy Utility" was in the August 26, 1968, edition. Luce's trials are covered in Lucy Komisar's "Con Ed: The Arrogance of Power" in the September 8, 1969, issue of *New York* magazine and get more sympathetic treatment from Susan Brownmiller in "Con Ed's Charles Luce, All Power (sometimes) to the People" that appeared in the March 17, 1970, *New York Times Magazine*. An insider's view of life in Con Edison's executive suite was given to me during an interview with William Wall, Con Edison's Vice President for Public Affairs, who spoke as one of the key new executives Luce had imported to help him out.

THE ROAD

Results from the various Hudson River studies I refer to are now becoming available, and those I used to improve my knowledge of the river, particularly its ecology, are: *Proceedings of the First Symposium on Hudson River Ecology* (Albany 1967) and *Proceedings of the Second Symposium on Hudson River Ecology* (Albany 1969). Perhaps the best short wrap-up on the river was done by Merril Eisenbud and Theo. Kneip of NYU's Medical Center, Institute for Environmental Medicine in their article, "Water Quality in Industrial Areas: Profile of a River," which appeared in the January, 1970, issue of *Environmental Science and Technology*. Dr. Kneip subsequently produced an interesting piece entitled "Sampling and Analytical Problems in a Complex Natural System: The

ACKNOWLEDGMENTS AND BIBLIOGRAPHY

Hudson River Estuary," which appeared in the December, 1971, issue of *American Laboratory*. The research on the river's ecology has become so active that the Hudson River Environmental Society, Inc. was formed in June, 1970, to coordinate what is going on. The Society may be contacted at P.O. 522, Tuxedo, New York 10987.

The dates, memoranda, and events that comprise the expressway story are taken from the files subpoenaed during the court case. Some of them have been conveniently assembled in the Hearings before the House Subcommittee on Fisheries and Wildlife Conservation held on June 24 and 25, 1969. I was able to draw on firsthand knowledge for some aspects of the expressway conflict. George Raymond, partner in the planning firm of Raymond, Parish, and Pine, helped me to understand the need for and impact of the expressway in the affected towns and villages. David Sive explained his participation and view of the case. He also gave me a copy of a paper entitled "An Environmentalist's Position" in which he outlined the significance of environmental litigation to the National Academy of Engineering. Joel Sachs of the Attorney General's Office in New York State gave me the state view of the expressway case. The briefs, court transcript, and decision were the written sources. Also helpful was Joseph Sax's account of the expressway conflict in "Defending the Environment: A Strategy for Citizen Action." "Prevention of Power Failures," a 1969 FPC report to the President, was a basic source for my comments on the blackout and "A Review of Consolidated Edison Power Supply Problems and Ten Year Expansion Plans" by the Bureau of Power of the FPC (1969) was my specific source for the present needs, problems, and plans of the Con Edison system.

Man and Atom: Building a New World Through Nuclear Technology (New York 1971) by Glenn T. Seaborg and William

ACKNOWLEDGMENTS AND BIBLIOGRAPHY

R. Corliss presents the case for nuclear power but without ignoring its dangers and problems. "The Future of Nuclear Power," a speech delivered on January 15, 1970 by Louis Roddis to the Science and Technology Advisory Council to the Mayor Of New York, summarized Con Edison's nuclear plans and problems. Doctors John W. Gofman and Arthur Tamplin of the Lawrence Radiation Laboratory have been among the more persistent critics of the AEC standards for nuclear plants and their case was presented on November 18, 1969, to the Senate Subcommittee on Air and Water Pollution. That the nation will rely on nuclear and fossil fuel generating plants for the foreseeable future seems to be the conclusion in "Environmental Effects of Producing Electric Power," Hearings Before the Joint Committee on Atomic Energy during October and November of 1969. The modest sums invested by the utility industry to find cleaner means of power production are listed in the research budgets, as of January, 1970, of the nation's 212 utilities, which appear in the January 28, 1970, issue of the *Congressional Record.* The utilities are spending eight times more on advertising than they are on research.

THE BRIDGE

The final FPC verdict on the Storm King plant was issued on August 19, 1970, the appeal briefs were argued on June 9, 1971, and the decision of the appeals court rendered on October 22, 1971. These formed the basic sources for my summary of the denouement of the case. My point that the FPC in 1971 was in some ways a different agency from the one that first licensed the plant is based partly on the broader sweep of the opinion as well as the changes in the plant design. Also significant, I felt, was the October 22,

ACKNOWLEDGMENTS AND BIBLIOGRAPHY

1970, staff brief on the hydro plant applications of the Pacific Northwest Power Company and the Washington Public Power Supply System recommending that these proposed Snake River projects, including one at High Mountain Sheep, not be licensed because of their harm to the scenery and aquatic life—the very arguments that Scenic Hudson had presented against Storm King. While the FPC is now more interested in environmental issues, its first priority remains power production, a message that comes through quite clearly in the testimony of John Nassikas, Chairman of the FPC, in his January 30, 1970, appearance before the Subcommittee on Energy, Natural Resources and the Environment of the Senate Commerce Committee. That steeply rising demand curves remain a key determinant of national energy policy is also made clear in the August, 1970, Report on Electric Power and the Environment sponsored by the Energy Policy Staff of the Office of Science and Technology.

The Los Angeles case I refer to is Department of Water and Power v. Hearing Board of the Air Pollution Control District of the County of Los Angeles, California Superior Court, Los Angeles County No. 97199, July 9, 1970. The question of thermal pollution seemed to be foremost in the minds of all the environmentally conscious Con Edison representatives I talked to. For a succinct and dispassionate analysis of that problem I relied on "Heat Rejection Requirements of the U.S.," by R. T. Jaske, J. F. Fletcher, and R. K. Wise in the November, 1970, issue of *Chemical Engineering Progress.*

My general acknowledgments start with Jack Macrae of Dutton whose enthusiasm, patience, suggestions, and continuing interest made this project a pleasure from start to finish. Marian Skedgell

ACKNOWLEDGMENTS AND BIBLIOGRAPHY

was an enormous help with her ideas for manuscript revisions and her skillful editing throughout. Dutton is a pleasant and efficient publisher to do business with and I want to thank everyone there who worked on the book.

My final but most important thanks goes to my family, especially to my daughter, Katharine Talbot, who is reaching the age where she is actually interested in the subject of this book and who submitted design suggestions which were incorporated in the book's cover. These are just some of the reasons I am dedicating this book to her.

INDEX

235

INDEX

INDEX

242

INDEX